Marvin Jones Memoirs

Congressman Marvin Jones with President-Elect Franklin D. Roosevelt, on the Roosevelt Train bound for Warm Springs, Georgia, January 21, 1933.

MARVIN JONES MEMOIRS

1917-1973
Fifty-Six Years of Continuing Service
in all Three Branches of the
Federal Government

Edited and Annotated by
JOSEPH M. RAY

TEXAS WESTERN PRESS
THE UNIVERSITY OF TEXAS AT EL PASO
1973

COPYRIGHT 1973
MARVIN JONES

Published By
Texas Western Press
The University of Texas at El Paso

ISBN 87404-038-8

Library of Congress Catalog 72-94877

In memory

of my mother

Docia Gaston (Hawkins) Jones

CONTENTS

Editor's Preface xi

I   *Home and Family* 1

II   *College* 9

III   *Law Practice* 14

IV   *Race for Congress* 22

V   *New Congressman* 31

VI   *Congress in Wartime* 35

VII   *Peace Comes* 40

VIII   *Postwar Congress* 45

IX   *The 1920 Election* 52

X   *Of Many Things* 56

XI   *Sidelights* 63

XII   *The Harding Administration* 68

XIII   *1928 and the Depression* 79

XIV   *The 1932 Campaign* 83

XV   *The President-Elect* 88

XVI   *The New President* 91

XVII   *The First Hundred Days* 98

XVIII	Soil Conservation and the Farmers' Share of the Tariff	104
XIX	The Frazier-Lemke Bill and Invalidation of AAA	115
XX	1936 Election — Pump Priming — Tenant Farmers	124
XXI	The Sugar Act	131
XXII	An All-Inclusive New Farm Bill	134
XXIII	Harvard University Studies New Farm Bill	138
XXIV	Last Days in Congress	142
XXV	Economic Stabilization	146
XXVI	The First International Food Conference	152
XXVII	War Food Administration	157
XXVIII	Judicial Service	163

Appendix I: Conclusion . 173

Appendix II: Vignettes . 180

Index 184

EDITOR'S PREFACE

I HAVE KNOWN of Marvin Jones since I first became aware of national politics. In my young manhood he was a national figure in Democratic politics during the administration of Franklin D. Roosevelt. I was aware both of his steadfastness and of his effectiveness in the nation's affairs. I first met him in Amarillo when I went there in 1957. My second encounter with him came in 1971 after he saw THOMASON: THE AUTOBIOGRAPHY OF A FEDERAL JUDGE and decided he would like his book, then in manuscript, to be produced as the Thomason book had been.

Marvin Jones' career in the public service far transcends my previous acquaintance with it. He was in Congress to vote on the declaration of the World War in 1917, and by the coming of the Democratic House Majority in 1931, he had fully earned his spurs. His performance in Congress during the historic years of the Roosevelt Administration is vividly recalled here. He started his long and distinguished judicial career in 1941 and is still at it as Senior Judge.

It would hardly be appropriate for me to attempt here to embellish this story. It stands on its own; it is a fine and significant book, and I am privileged to be involved in its publication. One of my principal contributions has been to reduce the length of the manuscript out of concern over the pricing of the finished book. I have performed substantial labors in preparing it for press, but the content, even the phrasing, are Judge Jones' own. He has been painstakingly involved in all editorial changes and annotations and he has guarded us against distortions and erroneous nuances of meaning.

The annotations following the Judge's comment on his judicial experience were necessitated by the traditional and understandable reticence of judges in speaking of their judicial performance. The earlier publication SHOULD UNCLE SAM PAY: WHEN AND WHY? is a selection of some of the Judge's opinions, without comment. The commentary included here attempts a brief evaluation of Judge Jones' judicial performance. The two appendices recommended *themselves to us as a more fitting method of summarizing a great man's career than if they had been in the Judge's own words. A commentator can tell the truth under such circumstances more forthrightly and with less inhibition than can the principal author.*

As publication time neared, misgivings arose with the author lest his relation of his life story appear unbecoming. Any person wishes to avoid appearing presumptuous in assuming a general interest in his story. In my opinion, he need feel no such concern. His long, rich, and productive life and his meaningful contributions in the legislative, executive, and judicial life of our nation over the last 56 years are here unfolded for your assessment. I think you will enjoy, profit from, and be instructed by this great man's recollections.

JOSEPH M. RAY

Marvin Jones Memoirs

Chapter I
HOME AND FAMILY

My mother and father were brought to Texas by their parents soon after Texas became a state. My father arrived in 1856, when Dallas was a village; Mother came a few years later. My folks lived in an area of Texas much of which was still unfenced. People branded their cattle and turned them loose on what was called the "commons." I can recall the times when farms were being fenced. Something of freedom seemed to be lost when the fences were built.

In those days the South was still suffering from the aftermath of the War Between the States. A civil war is the most terrible of all wars. The South was a broken country; it is the only country our nation ever defeated in war which was not taken by the hand and helped to its feet.

I was fourth in a family of eleven children, nine of whom lived to be grown, and four of whom — Herbert King (Hub) Jones and Frank Pierce Jones of Lubbock, Texas, and Mrs. Jeff M. (Metze) Neely of Amarillo, Texas, and I — are still living. I was born about twelve miles south of Gainesville, Texas, near the little town of Valley View. My father was a farmer at that time. He had operated a corn grinding mill and cotton gin as a young man, but he became a farmer after he was thirty and farmed most of the rest of his life.

My earliest memory was of an old-fashioned camp meeting, held in the woods on Spring Creek. I remember especially old-fashioned gas lights with open flames that flickered in the breeze.

A common custom in that region was leaving the home unlocked. People rarely locked the door even during two or three days' absence. On one visit to the home of my mother's parents, the trip home was delayed and we children were ravenously hungry. When we entered the house we found that someone had stopped there, cooked a meal and left a large breadpan half filled with beautiful brown, still warm biscuits. Despite our hunger, mother would not let us eat the biscuits because "they were not the right kind of people; it was all right for anyone to stop and prepare a meal for themselves in the empty house, but they were supposed to clean up, put everything back in place, and write a little note of thanks telling who they were." Wasn't that a beautiful custom?

We were permitted to have two dogs, but we always wanted more. Mother used to complain that every stray dog that came along decided to stay; what she did not know was that we would feed the animal out behind the barn or smokehouse. We had one dog that could climb a ladder and another that could jump into a wagon with extra sideboards while the team was in a sweeping trot. We had a cross-eyed cat that could catch a mouse without ever looking at it. We also had a one-eyed hen that had an uneven gait with a sort of side draft.

The farmers in our country grew about eight or ten different crops, principally wheat and cotton. Kafir corn, Indian corn, milo maize, sorghum cane, potatoes — both sweet and Irish — cantaloupes, and even peanuts, were all grown there. We wouldn't get through wheat harvesting and stubble plowing until cotton-picking time. About half through picking came the fall wheat-sowing and corn-gathering. Other crops would overlap, making year-around work.

We had plenty of fun hunting. At first we had an air rifle, then rifles, and finally shotguns. We hunted geese, ducks, quail and prairie chickens. Geese came over that country by the thousands.

People planning a party would pass the word at church on Sunday. For the most part the young folks would meet and sing and have their fun marching and swinging to their own music. The churches and school houses were the social centers. The young folks also had box suppers, fruit suppers, spelling matches and baseball. Box suppers, to be sold to the highest bidder, were offered by the young ladies. When a couple were badly smitten, someone would bid the box up high, knowing the boy would have to buy it. At the fruit suppers, the girls would bring cakes and boys would bring cans of fruit. When supper was announced, sweethearts would pair off, and then unattached boys and girls would form lines and be seated on opposite sides of tables. Tables were used in relays until all were fed.

We learned to ride cow ponies. At my first effort to cut a steer from the rest of the herd, the steer turned, the pony stopped stiff-legged, and I went over his head.

We did not have much time off. We worked from sunup to sundown when we weren't in school, doing the chores before sunrise and after dark six days a week. I decided I was not going to spend my life that way. Perhaps I was lazy. Somehow I sensed that education was the key to a different life.

In 1896 our house was completely destroyed by fire; only Mother and my second youngest sister were at home; the rest of us were in school a mile away. The neighbors took in the whole houseful of children until the home could be rebuilt. I stayed at the home of Mr. John Hancock, a veteran of the Texas Revolution, who was 93 years old. I tried to get the old man to talk about some of the battles that he took part in, but his hearing was not good and he did not like to talk. All he remembered was shooting and confusion.

The barn and some of the household furniture were saved from the fire, but most of the books were gone. We started building a new house right away. Some of the neighbors worked on the new house and gave pieces of furniture. Building a house did not cost so much since neighbors and even some of us children worked on it.

Our family read a great deal, and as a boy I was an avid reader. I read every book I could find on the Civil War. Three of my uncles and my father were in the Confederate army. I liked history; I read several books on Napoleon. I also read Cooper, Dickens, Mark Twain and Washington Irving. Dad always bought good books; if we read Dick Turpin or Frank Merriwell we had to do that on the sly.

One book that impressed me very much was a book I read before I was twelve years old, which told how man came from the soil and ultimately would go back to it; how when the nation's soil was wasted, the nation decayed. This book influenced my whole life and my life's work in Washington. It was burned in the fire and I do not remember the author or title.

Every little Texas community had a baseball team. When I was small we played town ball; we used a solid rubber ball less than half the size of a baseball. If a runner got off the base, we crossed him out by throwing the ball between him and the base. If we caught a batted ball on the fly or on the first bounce the batter would be out. Otherwise it was like baseball.

When baseball came along, we all took it up. Our family and a neighbor family, the Isbells, had an entire team. There was a deadly rivalry between the teams of the two small towns of Era and Valley View. The Era boys were big and strong, and they could hit the ball and run like jack rabbits. It was said that they would run alongside a jack rabbit, feel his sides to see if there was any meat on its bones, and if none was found, let the animal go. I don't vouch for the truth of this story. My long-time friend, Ewing Thomason, played baseball for Era. I heard Ewing make his first political speech in 1900; it was a great speech.

When the whole country is taking interest, talent is developed better than when there are scores of other competing forms of entertainment. There was no football except in the big colleges, and no basketball.

Until I was about sixteen, I went to a little country school called Elm Grove; the elms were long gone, but the name lasted. After Elm Grove, I went for one year to the little town school of Valley View. It's remarkable how much one learns from a good teacher; an outstanding teacher at Elm Grove was Miss Mary Carr. She made us want to learn; she inspired in most students a love of learning. We lived only a mile from school, and we walked to school; some pupils walked two and a half miles.

Our teacher believed in discipline; corporal punishment was administered, but usually it served the function of the musket behind the door. I am reminded of the story of the modern mother whose note to a teacher read, "Please don't slap Percy. He is very sensitive. Slap the boy next to him. That will scare Percy."

At nineteen, after one term in college, I taught at Elm Grove. It was a one-room school with nearly sixty students; I had classes in reading, writing, spelling, arithmetic, algebra, geometry, grammar, rhetoric, geography and history, with separate classes for different age groups — twenty-seven classes. I had to switch frequently from one class to the other. It was almost like a three-ring circus. The school was ungraded, as were most country schools in those days. I never attended a graded or high school. I took examinations to get into college; I have always felt that this College Board allowed something for my earnestness and determination.

General Lafayette, when he visited America in 1824, was a guest of my father's grandfather, James Edmonston Jones, on his plantation near Middleburg, Virginia. My grandfather became an invalid; from the age of sixteen, my father supported his father's family in the dark days following the Civil War. My dad taught me many things. He said I could ask more questions than anybody he ever saw, but he always answered them with patience and understanding.

All of the farmers we knew borrowed money to make their crops. They would usually pay ten percent interest taken out in advance and compounded every sixty or ninety days, with sometimes a little charge for making out the papers. You can see it would run up.

I went with my dad to the First National Bank in Valley View to borrow $250 on a ninety-day basis. As we left, I said, "Dad, why did you borrow money just for ninety days? We won't be able to pay it back for six to nine months." He replied, "The financial structure of this country is geared to the needs of industry and business and it is kept in what they call 'liquid condition.' There should be a separate credit structure suited to the needs of farm and livestock people, so they can produce a crop and produce cattle for the market."

I don't suppose that I was over ten years old, but those words were burned into my mind; therefore, when I ran for Congress the first time I used that idea as a plank in my platform. One of the first bills I introduced in Congress provided a separate credit structure for agriculture and I kept introducing it and talking about it. Shortly after Franklin D. Roosevelt became President we had the Farm Credit Act, which combined the five different types of farm and livestock credit; I have the pen with which President Roosevelt signed that bill. It was the culmination of a boyhood dream and a thinking farmer's philosophy.

I learned a great deal from my dad's interest in public affairs. He attended school only three months in his life. He read magazines, books and even school books; he helped me with my homework. He could have talked tariffs to the Tariff Commission. Senator Joe Bailey used to come to our home for dinner and we ate with him at the hotel in Gainesville when he came home from Washington, and he and Dad would discuss public questions. Dad had fully developed the wonderful art of conversation. People used to ask Dad where he went to college; he would answer with a smile that he never had that privilege; yet he read and studied all his life and in my book he was an educated man. He took a great interest in politics and government.

My father was a man of high principles. He once paid a seven dollar debt he didn't think he owed, because, he said, "I don't want any seven-dollar cloud hanging over me." When he had to, he would stand and fight; he wasn't afraid. He told me after I was elected to Congress, "It doesn't matter whether you make a great name, if you get a job done; that's the big thing. Don't worry about getting the credit, just do useful work. That's the source of strength in this country."

I was deeply gratified when I ran for Congress to discover how greatly he was respected by everyone who knew him. Time after time, as I ran for Congress from the vast fifty-three county district, people would say, "Are you the son of Horace K. Jones? Well, I don't know you, but I know him and I'll vote for you on his account." In the two German communities in my old home County of Cooke, a friendly physician told me, "You don't need to campaign here at Muenster or at Lindsay. They all know your dad, so you go campaign somewhere else." I got nearly all of the votes because of their confidence in my father.

My father was a member of the Methodist Church for over sixty years. He was the superintendent of the Sunday School and a steward in the Methodist Church for over forty years. He rarely missed a meeting. But he was tolerant in his religion as in all other things. To a degree, he integrated his economic and political ideas with those he read in the Bible. He said that history was built around human beings, that all Creation was built into a human being. He saw Bible facts as dovetailing with secular facts of life without conflict; he thought a man could live by principles and still be active in the business world.

He was in many respects a remarkable man. He settled many of the quarrels in the community. I asked him once, "Why do you try to settle these disputes? One side is always dissatisfied and sometimes both." He said, "Well, if I can settle a quarrel we can possibly avoid an expensive law suit and lasting hard feelings."

My mother was a Hawkins; she was born in Tennessee; her people came from the Carolinas. Her mother was Sarah (Sally) Gaston of Spartansburg, South Carolina, until her marriage to John Hawkins. One of her North Carolina relatives was William Gaston, who served in the State Senate, on the State Supreme Court and in the U.S. Congress, and was the author of the North Carolina State Song. His home in New Bern is preserved as an historical shrine. Three of my mother's great uncles fought in the American Revolution. Mrs. Thornton Gee wrote a history of the Gaston family; Gastonia, North Carolina, got its name from them.

Mother was always interested in public affairs and became intensely interested in politics. She and I watched the Conventions on television in Amarillo in 1948, when the Democrats nominated Harry Truman. I tried to persuade her to retire at her regular bedtime, because it would be 1:00 a.m. Texas time before Mr. Truman could make his acceptance speech. She said, "It does not make any difference, I want to hear all the speeches."

When she had heard Truman's stirring announcement that he and Alben Barkley were going to win, she said, "I believe Mr. Truman is going to be elected. I listened to the other man [Dewey] two weeks ago. He sounded as if he were a thousand miles away talking down to me. He didn't impress me at all. I think other people will react just like I did." At least on that occasion, Mother saw much farther into the future than most so-called experts.

She was born on July 6, 1856, and she died on December 28, 1958, almost six months after she became 102 years old.

Chapter II

COLLEGE

I HAD NEVER TRAVELED MUCH until I went to college. I did follow a schoolteacher to the Panhandle when I was about eighteen or nineteen years old and went to the public school in Miami, Texas, for one year. My brother and I attended Southwestern University in Georgetown, Texas, as youngsters right out of the country. One Monday we lugged our fabric telescope grips down the street of Georgetown toward the spire of the college building, and on out a country lane, winding up the college's back side. We climbed through the fence and literally entered college through the back door. The school had classes on Saturday and was off on Monday. Some of the students invited us to attend the meeting of a literary (debating) society. We stashed our luggage and went. They treated us as if we were special guests. Their thoughtfulness was greatly appreciated by two lads who were already beginning to be a little homesick.

Southwestern University, established in 1872, was the predecessor of Southern Methodist University, and its president, Dr. R. S. Hyer, became the first President of Southern Methodist. Southwestern had about 480 to 500 students. It could give more individual attention to students than could larger institutions.

There were several outstanding professors. President Hyer taught physics. He had experimented with wireless telegraphy for some years, sending messages several miles. Many thought he had probably perfected the invention before Marconi.

I learned in many ways at Southwestern, from other students as well as faculty. Some one has said that great teachers don't teach us much, but in their presence we are different people. There is much to be said for that statement; associations make the man. A young man develops differently if he spends all of his time in a library rather than in a pool hall.

I don't think that my character was greatly changed by the course I pursued. It had already been shaped in a fine home atmosphere.

My ambition was set a little by my discovery that I could compete with people no matter where they came from. After I had spent a few months at Southwestern University I was not afraid of anybody. I began to feel the thrill of accomplishment and purpose.

Part of my new self-confidence grew out of financing my own education. My father, a farmer with eleven children in days when farm prices were low, could not send his children to college. We earned all of our school money except for small loans from an old cattleman, Captain Larry W. Lee, of Valley View. When we had finished school, my brother and I each owed him about $250. I paid off my part of that note within about six or seven months after I started practicing law. When I went to pay my note and thank the Captain, he said, "Don't bother. I knew it was good all the time."

Each summer my brother and I canvassed the country, selling stereoscopes and slides showing beautiful scenes from all over the world. The first summer we started out afoot, carrying our canvassing case in Montague County, Texas. It required long hours of hard work, but we did well from the first. From the four summers' work we paid practically all our expenses in college and law school. And I think I learned more about human nature in the summertime than I did at college.

My brother and I both participated in debate activities. The two literary societies featured oratorical and declamation contests, and lyceum courses. I was chairman of the committee on lyceum courses, made the contracts for lyceum entertainment, handled the money for the sale of the tickets, paid the bills, and reported to the officials of the two societies.

The big event at Southwestern was the Brooks Prize commencement debate, which, in the absence of football, was the big event of the year. In 1905 J. E. Crawford and I were chosen to represent the San Jacinto Society against James N. Vincent and S. Young, representing the Alamo Society. It had been thought that one of the Alamo team would be my older brother Delbert (to provide a "battle of the brothers"), but the Alamo society chose Vincent instead.

We took the affirmative side of the topic, "Resolved: That Corporations Engaged in Interstate Commerce Should Be Required to Secure Federal Regulative Licenses." The house was packed with people and there were songs and yells and a great deal of enthusiasm. We won the decision by 4 to 1. As custom decreed, we presented the prize, a large number of books, to the college library.

I was the first baseman on the Southwestern baseball team in my last year. In the game against Baylor University, a base runner ran into me and hurt my wrist. I missed the first of three games at Fayetteville, Arkansas, against the University of Arkansas, with a swollen wrist.

A Mr. Wolfe, who was one of the directors of the Little Rock Club of the Southern League, bandaged my wrist so I could play. That day, when I came to bat with the bases loaded, I drove the ball out of the park. We won the game. Mr. Wolfe later asked me to try out for his club when my school year ended in June. He would give me a job between seasons paying $350 per month. I went home and asked Dad about it. Dad said, "If you want some career other than baseball, you would do better to go ahead with it, but it's your life and I want it to be your decision." I decided against a baseball career. Soon thereafter I made up my mind to go to the law school that fall.

When I was graduated from Southwestern in 1905, Vanderbilt University awarded me a scholarship; however, my brother and I decided to enter the Law Department of the University of Texas.

At the University of Texas a man was completely on his own. We had been required to attend church every Sunday at Southwestern. This religious atmosphere was less evident at the University of Texas. A man had to make his own way, with few people having a special interest in him. I am not sure that after a man reaches maturity, it isn't better to be in that environment. My brother and I were preparing for our profession, and we needed to stand on our own. We took extra courses and finished a three-year law course in two years.

Anybody who ever attended college can pick out a few men who helped to ignite the spark of his ambition. Such a man for me in the field of law was Dean Clarence Miller. The man who stood out from the standpoint of personal character was John C. Townes, then a professor and later Dean of the Law School. Both were exceedingly strong men.

During our senior year I won the Ross-Rotan prize in oratory — a gold watch that was given each year by Edward Ross of Waco, Texas, who had been a business partner of L. S. Ross, former Governor of Texas. The watch had a gold bust of Governor Ross riveted to the back of the case. My brother and J. D. Cobb represented the University of Texas the same year in the intercollegiate debate with the University of Missouri. My brother and I were chosen quizmasters for the following year.

I liked the study of the Constitution and corporation law more than any other subjects. We had one of the best men in corporation law that I have ever known, an instructor named Dr. Peterson. One afternoon Dr. Peterson wrote on the blackboard a brief statement of facts, then announced, "I want each of you to write an opinion of not more than fifty words, deciding this case. This is not an imaginary case; it was once decided by a divided court. I don't care how you decide it; I want to see whether you can find the exact point on which the case turns and not waste words on collateral matters." We usually had an hour to answer quiz questions, but he said, "Since this is new, you may take all afternoon." As soon as the students finished their opinions, many of them rushed to the library to run down the case to see how it was decided. This method was continued and the boys loved the course. Most of us felt it was the most effective course we had during our entire law student life. I sometimes wonder if all judges don't need a Peterson refresher course.

I am glad to note the tendency nowadays to teach practical things along with the theoretical and cultural. I have long urged law schools to require second-year students to work in the office of a clerk of a court or a successful law firm, even if they did nothing but carry books, attend trials and run errands. Even if they received no pay, it would be much less expensive than the second year of law school. Then the student could return to the law school and finish his course. In this way, the student would learn the practical and operative side of the profession, things he cannot be taught in school. Much of this same purpose is now accomplished by summertime jobs, which is probably more practical, if it could be required as a part of the course.

While I was quizmaster at the University of Texas, Dean Clarence Miller of the Law Department became ill, and I took charge of his classes in Constitutional Law and Partnership for the major part of a term. It was a fine experience; I learned much more about the subjects than I had learned in the classroom.

I resigned my position as quizmaster in April 1908, shortly after the near financial panic of 1907, and went to Amarillo, Texas, to practice law.

Chapter III

LAW PRACTICE

When my brother and I began seeking a location for the practice of the law, our father suggested Oklahoma City as the center of a land of great opportunity. We might have gone there if we had not been completely broke. We could have located in Gainesville, using Senator Joseph W. Bailey's law offices and library rent free.

My brother began practice in Dallas. I preferred the Panhandle of Texas, where I had lived for a year in Miami, and had fallen in love with its climate and with its independent and generous people.

Dean Clarence Miller at the University advised me to find a place where I would like to live and which held promise of good legal business; he urged me to take plenty of time in choosing my lifetime location. I visited Wichita Falls where there was a scarcity of lawyers, but then I heard that Leonidas C. Barrett, an Amarillo lawyer, wanted a young man in his office. I went there and called on him. After a brief talk we agreed on a week's trial run.

At the end of the week he called me in and told me that he would like to have me stay as a partner. He offered to pay all office expenses and give me twenty-five percent of the new business. I told him that was exceedingly generous, but that I would prefer fifteen percent of the new, five percent of any unfinished business I might be asked to work on, plus $25 per month. He responded, "That's not as good an offer as the one I made you." I said, "I know it isn't, but I can live on $25 a month and I want to be sure of a living." We closed the deal.

Soon after I began the practice of law, District Judge J. N. Browning appointed me as Special Master to audit the books and records in a lawsuit involving the purchase and several years' operation of the 137,000-acre Bravo Ranch. The Bravo, a part of the 3,000,000-acre XIT (ten counties in Texas) Ranch which had been traded in the early 1880's for the beautiful red granite State Capitol in Austin, had been jointly purchased several years before by H. B. Sanborn and O. H. Nelson. Sanborn had put up most of the money and Nelson had operated the ranch for eight years; now they were parting company, and I as master had to report to the court on thousands of cattle and all of the rest of the ranch's property. In the process I came to know two of the most colorful early Panhandle pioneers.

H. B. Sanborn was practically the founder of the present city of Amarillo. The owners of the land in the old village of Amarillo were asking high prices for lots. Sanborn laid out a townsite a mile away and offered free business and low-priced residential lots for construction. Practically the whole village moved to the new site, where Amarillo is now located.

Mr. Sanborn and Joseph Glidden of De Kalb, Illinois, were the joint inventors of barbed wire and secured the original patent. It was first known as Glidden Wire and was not immediately popular. There were many lawsuits by owners of injured cattle and horses. Mr. Sanborn told me that he sold his interest in the patent to Mr. Glidden for $25,000. Mr. Glidden made millions, but he endured many lawsuits. One of the main sections of Amarillo is the Glidden and Sanborn Addition. Mr. Sanborn had known "Billy the Kid," the notorious New Mexican outlaw, but had little respect for him.

O. H. Nelson was one of the first Texas cattlemen to bring high-grade cattle to the Panhandle. He told me an interesting story that I have retold many times.

The Oklahoma Panhandle is a narrow strip of land nearly 200 miles long, stretching above the Panhandle of Texas all the way to New Mexico. In the early days it was known as "Bad Man's Land." While Oklahoma was a territory, it became a haven for men who committed crimes in Texas, Arkansas, or Kansas. It was a common Texas saying that a fleeing criminal "has gone to the territory"; even the Federal Government usually did not bother to pursue them into the distant Oklahoma Panhandle.

Southwestern cattle were driven across this strip on their way to the market at Dodge City or Abilene, Kansas. Cowboys working on the drive were paid their accumulated wages when the cattle were sold. Most of them would blow in their money and then wander back toward home, across the strip, frequently alone or with one companion. While on the map the strip looks very narrow, it is more than 40 miles wide, more than a day's horseback ride.

The cowboys well knew the reputation of the strip. In looking for a place to spend the night, they looked for a dwelling where there was a garden or some flowers. They knew instinctively that a man, even a desperado, with sentiment enough to grow something with his own hands, would not harm a guest. If no such garden could be seen, the cowboy would ride on, hobble his horse, use his blanket for a bed, his saddle for a pillow, and sleep under the stars.

Judge Nelson assured me that this was not a fanciful story, but a part of the true history of that part of the country. Many years later as U.S. War Food Administrator, in addressing in Detroit a national convention of a thousand growers of war gardens, I told this story, because it seemed to fit the situation like a garment. After the speech scores of people complimented the wonderful story; my speech was almost lost in the story. Later at a Washington dinner party where I retold the story, a granddaughter of Judge Nelson identified herself to me; a few days later she took me to her home to meet her 92-year old mother, Judge Nelson's only daughter.

When I first practiced law in the Panhandle, the nearest court of appeals was in Fort Worth, nearly four hundred miles away. Shortly after my arrival an additional court of appeals was established in Amarillo to serve the sixty-nine counties of northwest Texas; its first session was held in 1910.

I argued case No. 1 in that court. It had been my law partner's case, but he was getting along in years and he wanted me to argue the case on appeal. It was an important judgment against the Santa Fe Railway. I really knew that case; I had read the record thoroughly and was well prepared. Scores of lawyers from around the area came to witness the opening of the court. It gave me an opportunity to become acquainted with them and also to appear when they all were present. It was a packed auditorium filled with lawyers from an area larger than most states. Afterwards, many lawyers asked me to brief and argue Court of Appeals cases. I appeared before that court nearly every Saturday for other lawyers from the area.

In 1913 the Judges on the Court of Appeals unanimously selected me as chairman of the Board of Legal Examiners for the counties in our area. I had not been an applicant and many others had applied, but the judges chose me anyway. I held that position for two and a half years.

I was told many law stories about the early days in the Panhandle by H. E. Hoover, a Santa Fe attorney at Canadian, Texas. Appealing an adverse decision was rare. Judge Sam H. Madden (the honorary title of "judge" is often informally bestowed in Texas on senior and prestigious lawyers) appealed the first case, and won; thereafter everybody wanted to appeal. Mr. Hoover told me of an old district attorney named L. D. Miller who tried a case in Ochiltree County, forty miles from the railway. The lawyer on the other side used some letters in evidence. L. D. Miller introduced a whole trunkful of letters, many of which had nothing to do with the case.

Miller lost and asked Mr. Hoover how to appeal. Hoover didn't want to miss the hack which was leaving soon for home. He told Miller, half in jest, "Put all of these letters in a tow sack, with the best ones on top, enclose a motion for a new trial, and mail the sack to the Supreme Court, Austin, Texas, in care of the Governor." Hoover said the case later appeared in the *Texas Reports* with a short opinion or order dismissing the appeal as not properly prepared.

In one case, I defended a man named Charles Merrit, who was crippled and used an artificial leg. He was indicted for assault with intent to commit murder. He had emptied his six-shooter from the sidewalk over a high picket fence at a man hoeing in a garden, but he had missed each time, for the man dropped the hoe and raced toward his back door. Merrit testified that his intended victim had disparaged his mother; the story was confirmed by neighbors. The district attorney was a vigorous prosecutor; I pleaded sudden impulse and emphasized the so-called unwritten law. I had hoped for an acquittal, but Charles feared he would get a long-term prison sentence. The jury stayed out for hours and finally brought in a verdict fining Charles $50. Charles was delighted, but I was somewhat disappointed. I later asked a member of the jury how they happened to fine my client $50. His reply was, "For being such a damn poor shot."

When a railroad kills a horse or a cow, the animal suddenly becomes a prized creature. Courts and juries understand this and usually discount inflated values. Lawyers also understand this and usually sue for more than actual value. I once met a shining exception to this practice. A man named Hall asked me to sue the Santa Fe Railway for killing his horse near Farwell, Texas. He said the horse was worth fifty dollars. I suggested that perhaps we had better ask for a hundred, since juries usually cut the claim in two. "No, sir," he replied, "I paid fifty dollars for that horse a short time ago; that's all he was worth."

I filed suit for $50, but soon thereafter my client moved to Memphis, Texas, about a hundred miles distant. Since it would cost my client something to come back to Amarillo, I told the company attorney I would recommend a $40 settlement, but he demurred, "Oh, no! I wouldn't pay you anything. This is one case I am going to win. That horse committed suicide. I have the proof." My adversary had taken the depositions of the engineer and fireman, both testifying that the horse had run at breakneck speed right into the rear drive wheel of the locomotive.

I was baffled, but I finally decided that the only course was to set the case for trial and ask Hall to come on to Amarillo. When I told him of the new testimony, to my astonishment he said, "Oh, that was Mr. Barton's horse. That horse was killed about 150 yards north of where my horse was killed. The train was running at terrific speed. It did not stop at the little town of Farwell." I said, "Are you willing to swear to those facts?" "Sure," he said, and he gave me the names of local people who knew of the two horses being killed. I decided not to ask for a jury. On the stand, Hall's story could not be broken. The defense counsel asked for a continuance but the judge denied it, saying, "I am convinced this man is telling the truth. Judgment for the plaintiff in the sum of $50."

I once tried a case in Plemons, the county seat of Hutchinson

County. Joe Ownby, the manager of the Turkey Track Ranch, attended the trial; a few days later Joe Ownby called on me in Amarillo and I secured a very valuable client, The Turkey Track Ranch.

Ownby had been driving a large herd of cattle from near Bovina to the main ranch in Hutchinson County, about 150 miles northeast. The weather was very dry, and the cattle spotted a large pond inside a pasture and could not be stopped. After they had their fill, they were quite docile again.

In a short while Ownby was arrested and taken before the Bovina Justice of the Peace. The Justice of the Peace made him put up a $200 cash bond on a trespass charge and entered a suit in favor of the pasture owner in his court for $5,000 damages, actual and punitive. Apparently, he treated the $200 as a sort of criminal penalty for trespass. Ownby had to put up the $200 because he could not leave the cattle in charge of inexperienced hands. He put up the bond, drove the cattle on to the ranch, and came back to my office. We drove down to Bovina and went before the Justice of the Peace who was rather arbitrary and demanding. He refused to impanel a six man justice court jury until the next day. I asked for a few minutes to consult with my client, and took Ownby outside and asked him to stand by me while I tried to scare the Justice of the Peace.

I went back and said to the Justice of the Peace, "I plan to appeal to the County Court any judgment you render. In the meantime, you have accepted a lawsuit for $5,000 damages when the limit of your jurisdiction is a suit for $200. I also plan to file a damage suit against you for $10,000 in the District Court for attempting to utilize powers far beyond your jurisdiction, and I am also going to join your bondsmen as joint defendants."

This speech rather scared my client, but the Justice of the Peace promptly became tractable; he didn't want any kind of a lawsuit, especially one that involved his bondsmen. He offered to settle for a $50 fine, and when I refused, he lowered it to $20. I still refused, although my client was sitting there wanting me to accept. I finally agreed to a $1 fine, and Mr. Ownby got his $200 back, less the costs of the court and the sheriff's mileage traveled in the service of papers in the case.

On the way back to Amarillo, Ownby said he wanted me to represent Turkey Track Ranch regularly. We agreed on my fee, and after that, until I fell from grace and got into politics, I represented the Turkey Track Ranch.

There was not much timber in the Panhandle of Texas, but part of the Turkey Track Ranch was in the breaks of the Canadian River in which there were a considerable number of cottonwood trees. To get there, I took the railway to the town of Panhandle and then caught the mail hack for the forty miles to Plemons, where Joe Ownby met me with a surrey and two good horses for the drive out to the ranch headquarters.

It was a wonderful old place. On each side of the roadway into the ranch headquarters was a row of beautiful giant cottonwood trees. In those days, practically all of the ranches in the Panhandle were located where there were springs and continuous running water. With water available for irrigation, the ranch headquarters was in a fine setting and looked very beautiful to me. After we had disposed of the business I had come for, Joe Ownby would drive me back to Plemons to catch the mail hack back to town.

Once when we arrived back in Plemons, an immense crowd had gathered around the courthouse. I learned that a man had been charged with bootlegging and he wanted an attorney. I had to meet the mail hack in three hours and I did not think I would have time to represent him. I had never defended a bootlegger, but I agreed in this case on the promise of the owner of the mail hack to wait if necessary until we finished that trial. The issue was whether the accused would be placed under bond or jailed awaiting the action of the grand jury.

The Justice of the Peace, a bright and personable young man, in the absence of a prosecuting officer acted also as district attorney and examined eighteen of the nineteen witnesses called; one had failed to appear. Each witness testified that he had gone to a camp across the Canadian River and had been told to turn his back and face the river and then to flip a dollar over his shoulder. When he did this, a bottle of whiskey fell down by his side. On cross examination, each witness said he did not know who got the dollar, did not know where the whiskey came from, and did not see anyone place the whiskey beside him.

When the State's witnesses had finished, the Justice of the Peace invited my argument. I declared at the beginning that the State's testimony was wholly insufficient; not a single witness testified that he paid the defendant any money; and no witness had positively identified my client. I argued that a man cannot be convicted on suspicion, because the principle that a man is presumed innocent until proved guilty by competent evidence beyond a reasonable doubt has been woven into the law since the beginning of organized government. I made as strong a plea as I could for about twenty-five minutes.

When my argument was finished, the Justice of the Peace declared, "One of the nineteen witnesses that were summoned for testimony in this case has failed to appear. I fine him $25, and I intend to make it stick." He spoke so positively I began to fear for my client, but to my surprise he continued: "I think the State of Texas has gloriously failed to make out a case, and the defendant is discharged."

The accused took the money for my fee out of a big pound tobacco sack, stuffed full of money. I advised him, "This is not the end of the case. The grand jury can still indict you and it likely will. You should get out of Texas and not come back within the statute of limitations (then two or three years)." He responded, "I'll leave before the sun goes down." That was the only bootlegger I ever defended as a trial lawyer.

Another of my favorite law stories has been written up in the history books. It was told to me by a famous lawyer, then retired, who had practiced law in the Indian Territory in Oklahoma. Federal judges in the Territory were appointed by the President. One such judge, a man named Hastie, was well equipped with common sense. Someone sued in his court to recover on a note bearing interest of two percent per month. The defendant's lawyer pleaded usury. The plaintiff countered that there was no law against usury in the Territory. The judge agreed with the latter point, and added, "But there is a law against highway robbery, and that's what this is. The plaintiff will be allowed only the conventional rate of interest."

Chapter IV

RACE FOR CONGRESS

&§ I CAN SCARCELY REMEMBER a time when I was not interested in politics. I made up my mind as a schoolboy that I would run for Congress at the first opportunity. Once when I returned home after being away several days, I came across the pasture to the back end of our field where some of my brothers and sisters were working. My brother Hub asked me where I was going, and I replied, "I am going to Congress." They made quite a joke of it, but, while I spoke facetiously, I had Congress in mind even then. It may seem strange that an unsophisticated youngster wearing patched trousers should harbor such ideas. But in this free and fruitful country that is just what young people do. It is perfectly natural in a land where there is freedom from every form of caste and privilege and where the tyranny of wealth and birth has never been allowed to close the door of opportunity in the face of any citizen.

I have always thought that the priceless privilege of living in the clear atmosphere of the open country, leaning against a fodderstack, chewing a straw, and engaging in uninhibited daydreaming about the future is the great gift of life and is almost as essential to any growing boy as his food and raiment. It's all right to dream if you don't go to sleep.

In my youth, the Fifth Congressional District of Texas was represented by Joseph W. Bailey, who was elected to Congress when he was twenty-eight and became Democratic Floor Leader in the House when he was thirty-four, after only six years of service. My friend Sam Rayburn and I were both reared in his district, and as long as Joe Bailey lived he took a great interest in both our careers. For this reason I think it appropriate to tell something of him and his remarkable personality.

Just before the turn of the century, when Thomas B. Reed of Maine was Speaker, Congressman Bailey was Floor Leader in the House. At that time the Speaker had almost complete control of everything. On one occasion Bailey had a specific agreement with the Speaker as to when a certain bill would be taken up, but for some reason the Speaker changed plans and brought up another bill instead. Bailey openly charged the Speaker with violating his word.

Quite an uproar ensued. The newspapers throughout the country published the pictures of both men and made much of the story. Bailey was very popular in Gainesville. A mass meeting was called by State Senator C. L. Potter to pass some resolutions of commendation to send to the young Congressman Bailey. The chairman of the meeting appointed a committee to draft resolutions. While the committee was out preparing a draft, a number of stirring speeches were made, and the crowd became somewhat enthusiastic. When the proposed resolutions were read they were composed largely of a simple statement of facts followed by a commendation of the courageous action by the Floor Leader. Some in the crowd thought the resolutions too prosaic; they wanted a more fulsome resolution.

In the audience was a keen lawyer by the name of William O. Davis. He and Bailey for some reason disliked each other. Each took every possible occasion to make cutting remarks about the other. Attorney Davis always attended these pro-Bailey meetings. At that time Congressman Bailey wore his hair rather long, and it always tumbled down close to his collar. He was a very distinguished-looking man. Davis rose, addressed the chair, and offered to propose a resolution for the consideration of the meeting.

The Chairman knew that Davis was not a friend of Congressman Bailey, but he could see no reason why Davis should not be allowed to present the resolution. Davis stated his resolution was in the form of a telegram, which could be immediately sent to Congressman Bailey. He then read, "Dear Joe: Cut your hair and come home." It almost caused a riot. Many screamed, "Throw him out!" But Davis had gotten in his lick and was perfectly happy.

Davis also always attended the public speeches of Congressman Bailey. Bailey would talk to his home folks about various public issues and sometimes about matters of local and personal interest. On one of these occasions he said: "One of my friends asked me one time why I did not join the church and become a Christian. I replied I could not do this for two reasons. First, if I made any commitments along this line I would have to preach, since I would be impelled to devote any talent I may have to man's greatest calling. In the second place, I would have to forgive old Bill Davis, and I couldn't do that."

I made up my mind in 1912 to run for Congress at the earliest opportunity, which would be in 1914. However, in July 1913, William E. Prescott, a County Judge, announced early as a candidate in 1914. I felt that it would be very difficult to defeat the incumbent, John H. Stephens, if two candidates ran against him and therefore decided to defer my candidacy until 1916. Prescott was defeated decisively, but he promptly confounded my plans by announcing the next day his intention of running in 1916. I decided to run in 1916 anyway.

The Thirteenth Congressional District had 700,000 people — more than enough for two congressional districts. There were eight or ten prospective candidates waiting for redistricting in order to run for Congress. I decided it would be easier to beat Stephens and Prescott in the big district than all the others in a smaller district, so I became the first candidate to file formally in the 1916 primary. Stephens and Prescott also announced, along with Reuben M. Ellerd, a wealthy former district attorney.

My formal announcement for Congress was made at Amarillo. Bascom Timmons, a reporter on the newspaper, wrote an editorial about my candidacy. I bought a Model T, got some literature, and started out to visit the various towns and cities all over the district. I began with a hand-shaking campaign, attending all picnics and public gatherings, and visiting some of the public schools.

In the spring mornings, I would drive the car up to the likeliest looking corner and park, unsnap the top of my Model T Ford, and walk around the town telling everybody I was going to speak in a few minutes and would appreciate their coming to hear me. Sometimes I would start with only a half dozen present, but the most of the town would be there eventually, since there wasn't much going on in the morning in those little towns. I would finish speaking, shake hands, and go on to the next town and do the same thing. In the afternoon, the farmers would be in town; they would usually attend, while businessmen would stay in the stores. I often made seven or eight short speeches a day that way.

I remember well my visit to the little town of Dundee. I had spoken earlier at Seymour, and had not eaten much breakfast, and I was to speak at Wichita Falls in the afternoon. In Dundee at noon I asked a groceryman if there was a hotel or a restaurant in town. He pointed out a little restaurant across the street. I walked over to the restaurant and found it locked. When I told this to the storekeeper, he said, "Oh, I forgot to tell you, he locks up and goes home for dinner every day." I sat down in the back of the grocery store and ate some cheese and crackers with two or three other fellows. I had never before known of a man running an eating place who closed it up to go home to dinner.

There were only eleven miles of paved highway in the entire district; I would get stalled in the sand with that old Model T or get in the river and have to be pulled out. If you went five hundred miles before you got a puncture, you'd brag about it for a week; they hadn't yet discovered carbon black to toughen tires, and tires did not last as long as they do now.

I once spoke at a big barbecue picnic in Matador, the county seat of Motley County. There were a good many mesquite trees, but they didn't give much shade. A great long arbor had been built and covered with gunny sack material — big enough to hold a big crowd — with a speaking stand on one side. The arbor provided the only available shade, and all of the men, women, and children spent most of their time there.

Just across from the speaker's stand was the loudest mechanical musical instrument I ever heard, playing for a merry-go-round drawn by a pair of rabbit mules. Dr. S. P. Brooks, president of Baylor University and running for the United States Senate, spoke that morning. He was a wonderful speaker, but nobody could hear him because of the noise made by the merry-go-round. One of my opponents, Reuben M. Ellerd, spoke first in the afternoon. He wore his voice out trying to make people hear him, but very few did.

While Ellerd was speaking, I asked Wendell Johnson, with whom I had been to college, to try to hire the merry-go-round operator for about three dollars to break down when I started speaking. He came back grinning and said, "I got him for two." I had a magnificent audience; those country people wanted to hear speaking, and they had not had anyone that they could hear. Ellerd said later, "You're the luckiest damned man I ever saw." He probably never knew.

Congressman John H. Stephens was in 1916 Chairman of the Committee on Indian Affairs. I told the people I had no prejudice against Indians, but in the fifty-three counties in the District I had found only one Indian, a wooden Indian in front of a cigar store at Fifth and Polk Streets in Amarillo. I assured people that if I went to Congress I would get assigned to some committee in which my people at least would have a direct interest. At no time did I criticize John H. Stephens personally. However, I did tell the following incident.

One morning when I was a country school boy in Cooke County, a buggy drawn by a fine team of horses drove up to the schoolhouse. The driver came into the schoolhouse and our teacher introduced him as Congressman John H. Stephens. I am sure he made a good speech, but the thing I remembered most went something like this: "Young men, within a few years, older men are going to step aside and you young men are going to take our places. The people of this country are just and fair. All you need to do is to study hard and equip yourselves, and the American people will honor you with any position you are qualified to fill." Then I would add, "I remember those words vividly. I finished my course, worked my way through college and began to practice law. I have no criticism of Mr. Stephens, but I am just reminding him of what he said twenty years ago."

I drove my Model T Ford about thirty thousand miles. I covered the district from Lewisville, Texas, thirty-five miles from Dallas, to Dalhart, more than four hundred miles away. I visited every community and tried to meet all the people. I spoke anywhere a group could be got together. Congressman Stephens and I spoke from the same platform on three occasions, but he refused to debate me. He was probably wise, because it would have given extra advertising to his unknown opponent. Senator Joseph W. Bailey once refused to debate an opponent, saying, "I don't propose to kick him into celebrity."

On one occasion I was to speak at a picnic in Goree, but I arrived late. It was hot and many of the people were leaving, but those who remained insisted that I should speak. Nearby stood the circus tent of Mollie Bailey, who for twenty-five years operated a traveling one-ring circus all over the Southwest. A friend told me that the circus performance was about over and he was sure Mollie would let me speak in her tent. We went to see her, and found her quite agreeable. Not only could I use the tent, which provided the only shady place around there, but she would roll up the outside curtains and would even announce the speech before the last act. She did just that, and I had a marvelous audience.

I made some three hundred speeches in the campaign, many of them brief. Longer speeches were made at picnics and at scheduled times in the evening or on Saturday afternoon. I found it good politics to visit livery stables, wagon yards, and barbershops, since these were places where people in all walks of life met and talked.

I came to realize the value of using the terminology of any man's profession when I first met him. I had learned much about blacksmithing as a farm boy. I walked into a little blacksmith shop at a small village called Wizzard Wells, about thirty miles from Decatur. As I talked to the blacksmith, he became interested, and said he would be glad to vote for me. About ten days later, I spoke at a big picnic at Decatur; after the speech, several people asked, "Have you seen that blacksmith who came thirty miles? He says you are the only man in the United States he would drive thirty miles to hear." The only time I ever met him was the few minutes in his blacksmith shop, but I have always remembered him as a helpful friend.

The occasion in Decatur was a four-day reunion picnic held annually and attended by thousands. A family named Short camped for the entire four days with children and grandchildren; they asked me to dinner. The five boys were all for me but their father was for Stephens. After dinner a fourteen-year-old granddaughter named Violet wanted to get a picture of me and her grandfather, but he balked. I urged him to come on, promising I wouldn't tell Mr. Stephens, and our picture was taken with him in his shirt sleeves. When the election was over and I had won, Violet sent me a copy of the picture of "the two greatest men in the world — my grandfather and our Congressman." She wrote that her grandfather said if he had known I was going to win he would have put on his coat. Violet Short later became a distinguished writer.

One of my opponents in the race was Reuben M. Ellerd of Plainview. He had a great deal of ready money, and he spent it freely. He took an ad practically every week in each of the 106 country newspapers in the big district. At a schoolhouse, he would pass out three or four hundred pencils with his picture on them. He gave away a game for children called "Table Quoits." He distributed celluloid cards with a map of the district. He also mailed from Plainview sixty thousand calendars printed in twelve different colors.

Ellerd had several other men going over the district making speeches for him; one of them was a preacher named Hardy. He was a very fine speaker; I had heard him preach at a "protracted meeting" when I was a boy at Valley View. On July 17, seven days before the primary, the people of Tulia held their annual picnic commemorating the founding of the town. I attended the picnic. Ellerd was not there, but the Reverend Hardy was there to look after Ellerd's interests. He brought calendars, pencils, and table quoits for children. We spoke in the Courthouse. He spoke first, boasting about what Ellerd was giving the people, and twitting me for giving them nothing except my card.

When I arose I told of hearing Reverend Hardy preach at Valley View, and then I added, "In those days Reverend Hardy seemed to be called of the Almighty to preach the unsearchable riches of the Gospel, but this year he seems called of Reuben Ellerd to distribute pencils and calendars." He turned very red and the people almost raised the roof in laughter and applause. I continued, saying, "I never thought it was quite proper to offer anything of value when seeking votes. Mr. Stephens gives you garden seeds; Mr. Ellerd gives you pencils and calendars; but I'll give you a Congressman if you will elect me."

During the campaign, Europe was aflame with war, and America was very much concerned. One of the arguments most effectively used against me was that I was too young, that the district needed a man of mature judgment. I quoted Champ Clark's remarkable speech in which he said a man had to learn to be a Congressman just as he had to learn to be a blacksmith, a lawyer, or a doctor; that it took several years to learn the machinery of that great body; that a man older than fifty should not be elected to Congress for the first time; and that most noted congressmen started before they were forty.

During the last month of the campaign, one of my brothers, who was just out of college, drove the car for me. About 8:30 one evening we came upon a new town entirely surrounded by barbed wire; we finally found a gap at one corner and drove inside. The only light in town was at a camp meeting; we attended the meeting and when the preaching was over I introduced myself to one of the men and told him we wanted to find a place to sleep. He said, "There's no hotel here; it's a new town; we have it fenced in to keep the cattle from bothering us. You can stay at my house; I'm postmaster here, and I've got the post office in my front room. You can sleep in the post office." We slept on pallets in the post office of Dumont.

Reuben Ellerd's lavish spending provided grist for many of my speeches. I insisted that Americans didn't want their Congress to be a rich man's club like the British House of Lords. Most wealthy men want to be fair; it is their money, and they have a right to spend it as they please. But no one wants to close the door of opportunity to every young man of ordinary means.

I had been embarrassed many times by candidates urging me to promise to vote for them. I never asked anyone to make a direct commitment. I would tell him my name, what I was running for, and express appreciation for any help or support he could give me, all without asking for an answer. Occasionally someone would speak up and say he would vote for me, and I would thank him, but I doubt that these amounted to more than three percent of the people I met.

I went back to my home town to spend the day of the election, July 22, 1916. Even though local polls taken in many parts of the district were favorable, I was naturally somewhat anxious. Within a short time returns showed me in the lead; when they were complete, I had carried all but five of the counties, and I had received as many votes as all the other three men together. I felt an overwhelming humility. Democrats in Texas in those days outnumbered the Republicans by about ten to one, and victory in the Democratic primary was tantamount to victory in the general election. I did no campaigning at all after I won the primary.

My campaign expenses, including the cost of the car, gasoline, oil and other travel and printing expenses, totaled less than $2,000. I spent six months of individual work, almost day and night. In these days of television, radio and paid workers, running for office is much more expensive than it was in 1916.

Chapter V

NEW CONGRESSMAN

THE YEAR 1916 was an exciting year — a great world war was going on in Europe. Germany had overrun Belgium and a large part of France. Charles Evans Hughes had resigned from the Supreme Court, after being nominated as Republican candidate for President against Woodrow Wilson, who was seeking a second term. Since I had just been nominated for Congress by the Democrats in the 13th District of Texas, I was requested by the Democratic National Chairman to speak in other states in behalf of the national ticket. I campaigned in several Southwestern states.

Wilson's campaign slogan for reelection was "He kept us out of war." The election was extremely close. It was first thought that Hughes had won. The final vote in California, which was not completely tabulated until two or three days after the election, tipped the scales in favor of President Wilson.

Early in 1917, the German government established a war zone across the Atlantic Ocean and declared its intention to sink any vessel bearing arms that came into that zone. German U-boats were sinking many English vessels. The announcement of such a zone caused a storm in the Congress. Some wanted to warn Americans to stay out of the zone; others felt no nation could abridge the traditional freedom of the seas. Germany began carrying out its declared purpose. The President declared he would wait for the actual sinking of an American vessel, and some were sunk.

I arrived in Washington in December 1916; the new Congress did not convene until March 4, and the old lame duck session still had three months to go. I came up early to attend a freight-rate case before the Interstate Commerce Commission and to familiarize myself with Washington.

Texas had a higher freight rate schedule than most Southwestern states and the Panhandle Plains had an even higher rate structure. The two cases were combined. Mr. Burney of Ft. Worth, employed to argue both cases, placed his entire argument on the all-Texas rates, and made no reference to the Panhandle's dilemma. Mr. J. R. Jackson, of Amarillo, and I approached a member of the Commission and asked that I be given ten minutes to present our problem. The permission was readily granted.

I stated to the Commission that we joined heartily in asking the entire rate structure of the state be reduced, but that we had a special problem. Our section of Texas was now much more thickly populated than when the higher rates were fixed. I mentioned that I now represented more than 700,000 people. When the decision came down, the higher West Texas rate structure was removed but the all-state application was temporarily denied. About two years later the entire rate structure was reduced.

I spent about a month in Washington getting acquainted and studying legislative procedure. As a newly elected member, I had the privilege of the floor even though I had not become an actual member. One day while I was sitting there by myself in the House, Speaker Champ Clark left his chair and came and sat down by me. We talked for about thirty minutes. He advised me to write out every point of order that comes up and then later look up all of the precedents; in that way, he predicted, I would soon know more about the rules of the House than most members. I followed his advice.

Speaker Clark told me that the best time for a man to come to the House was in his youth, because it took time to learn the legislative process; once the younger man has learned this process, said the Speaker, he can represent his constituents better. He said a man needs to learn the operation while he is still young, vigorous and ambitious.

Much of that lame duck session was taken up with war legislation. President Wilson had recommended "preparedness" legislation and there was a great deal of controversy over some of his measures. During this period, President Wilson had referred to the "little group of wilful men" who had prevented the passage of some of his recommended legislation. The Congress adjourned the short session on March 4, 1917.

President Wilson called an extraordinary session of the Congress to meet April 2, 1917. It was agreed that the two houses would meet in joint session at 8:30 in the evening of April 2 to receive the President's message. It was an exciting session. The gallery was packed. Nearly all the members were present. While we were waiting for the President, a woman threw a banner over the side of the gallery opposing our entry into the war. The guards confiscated her banner and ejected her.

When the President walked in, everyone stood and cheered. He read the war message. It was a magnificent message dramatically delivered and repeatedly applauded. He was given a standing ovation when he finished. Identically worded Senate and House Joint Resolutions were introduced, declaring in effect that a state of war existed with the Imperial Government of Germany. The House Foreign Affairs Committee conducted hearings on April 3 and reported the Resolution favorably the late afternoon of April 4. The House met at 10 o'clock the morning of April 5.

I was deeply impressed with the President's message, but no one wanted to go into war. Even those who voted for it did so reluctantly. The House debated the War Resolution long and earnestly. There was considerable opposition in the country to sending an army abroad. There was much more talk in the cloakroom than on the floor in opposition to a declaration of war.

Claude Kitchin, the Democratic floor leader, made a strong speech against the War Resolution, and urged negotiation and delay. Swager Sherley of Kentucky, on the other hand, thought we had no choice. About six that evening I told John Garner that I had heard many doubts expressed. He said, "That's just talk. When the roll is called there won't be over fifty votes against the President on this resolution."

The Foreign Affairs Committee had previously held a secret hearing, then reported the resolution, recommending its passage. The debate had begun in the morning, lasted through the day and without intermission until 3 o'clock the next morning. The members of the committee refused at first to reveal what the evidence before them had been, because it was classified information. Many members of the House complained bitterly. Finally, well into the evening, Henry Allen Cooper of Wisconsin, a member of the Committee, disclosed what the hearings had revealed, saying that the members were entitled to know the facts before being required to vote on a resolution of such tremendous importance.

It was a tremendously interesting debate. Inspiring speeches were made by members of the Foreign Affairs Committee and by Finis Garrett of Tennessee, who soon thereafter became Democratic leader. There were only fifty votes against the war resolution. The first lady to be elected a member of the House, Jeanette Rankin of Montana, voted "no." Press reports indicated that she cried and did not vote, but this was incorrect. I sat right across the aisle from her; when her name was called, she stood and said in a low voice, "I want to stand by my country but I cannot vote for war. I vote 'no'." A House rule forbids explanation of a vote during roll call. A roll call takes more than forty-five minutes; if explanations were permitted, it would last forever.

I went over to the Senate to listen to some of their debate on the War Resolution. Some interesting speeches were made; Ollie M. James made a wonderful ten-minute speech; several spoke against the Resolution. The Senate Joint Resolution was duly passed; in the House it was substituted for the House Resolution and passed early in the morning of April 6, 1917. The President signed it as soon as it reached him the morning of April 6, 1917.

Chapter VI

CONGRESS IN WARTIME

ALMOST IMMEDIATELY bills to implement the war began to come before the House. Opposition to these measures caused considerable controversy. One of the first bills appropriated $50,000,000 to enable the President to act in emergencies. Claude Kitchin brought in a measure with a proposed graduated income tax rate ranging to a top bracket of sixty-five percent, an unheard of rate; under his sponsorship the bill was overwhelmingly passed.

The decision was made to sell bonds directly to the people. Theretofore government bonds had usually been absorbed by banks and by mortgage and insurance companies. If people could be induced to buy bonds as a patriotic duty, it would bring the public more strongly behind the war. A four billion dollar bond issue was planned and Claude Kitchin sponsored it.

William Schley Howard of Atlanta wanted to amend "The Liberty Loan Bill," to reduce the $50 denominations to $1. Kitchin responded that it would take more to print dollar bonds than the year's interest would bring. When the vote was taken, there wasn't a single vote for the amendment; even Howard did not vote for his own amendment. The Treasury later devised the War Savings Stamps to paste in books and accumulate toward bonds.

Claude Kitchin told of an instance when he was doing yard work in his overalls at his home in Scotland Neck, North Carolina, when a lady came asking for Mrs. Kitchin, who was not at home. In response to the lady's insistent questioning Kitchin revealed he worked there and had done so for about twenty-five years, and that his only pay was his board and clothes. The lady exclaimed, "My good man, don't you know that is peonage?" Mr. Kitchin smilingly replied, "That may be what you call it up North, but down here we call it matrimony."

The drive to sell government bonds to individuals on a mass basis was an unheard of feat. Many said it could not be done. A famous writer once said that a man who says a thing cannot be done is usually interrupted by someone doing it. William G. McAdoo, the Secretary of the Treasury, was placed in charge. George Creel, a famous writer, was made director of publicity. A date was set for the kick-off and Marie Dressler, Douglas Fairbanks, Mary Pickford and Charlie Chaplin were brought to Washington. Their coming had been highly advertised. I heard all four of them make speeches; Marie Dressler was a tremendous speaker, but all of them made effective talks. Charlie Chaplin, as always, brought down the house in screams of laughter. The Liberty Loan was oversubscribed.

There was a great deal of debate on the proposal to make all young men between the ages of 18 to 21 years subject to the draft. When the Chairman of the Military Committee refused to support the bill, the President asked Julius Kahn, a Republican from California, to manage the bill on the floor. A large majority of the members on both sides of the aisle preferred a voluntary plan. The debate lasted three weeks. Those in charge of the bill were wise in not bringing it to an early vote.

Speaker Champ Clark opposed the draft. His was the best speech against passage. He commented facetiously that during the Civil War the people of Missouri saw little difference between a conscript and a convict. Newsmen distorted this as a direct statement by him. I made my first speech before the House in favor of the draft, on the theory that the whole issue was determined when we voted on the war resolution. Level-headed Sam Rayburn declared in the cloakroom that he would not vote for the draft, even if 90 percent of his people voted for it. Later, when he changed his mind, someone twitted him, saying, "Sam, didn't you say that you wouldn't vote for the draft even if ninety percent of your people favored it?" "Yes," he said, "but ninety-five percent of my people favor it." The measure passed by a wide margin.

During a drought period, I worked with Senator John Kendrick of Wyoming, a former Texan, to secure a temporary reduction of freight rates on cattle feed. We also secured an extension of the low rates when the drought continued.

Asbury Frank Lever, Chairman of the House Committee on Agriculture, handled the Lever Food Bill of 1917. Up to that time, we had never had price-fixing. History has laughed at price-fixing and mocked the price-fixer; but in wartime people will accept many things that would be rejected in normal times. There was a tremendous fight over Frank Lever's bill. He was a clever floor manager and a brilliant speaker. His bill became the basis of the War Food Administration headed by Herbert Hoover. Jim Young of Texas managed to get cotton exempted from the bill. Then the wheat people got an amendment stipulating that the price of wheat should not be fixed at less than two dollars a bushel. Lever emphasized that the bill covered only food, feed, and fuel. Months later it was finally passed after many amendments.

For many years there had been a growing sentiment for national prohibition of the manufacture and sale of intoxicating liquor. The Prohibition Amendment was submitted to the states for ratification on December 17, 1917; it was ratified by the states as the Eighteenth Amendment on January 16, 1919. I voted to submit the amendment. I believed in it at the time. Wayne B. Wheeler of the Anti-Saloon League usually sat in the House Gallery when the amendment was under consideration.

When I was a schoolboy, our teachers taught us the evils of alcohol. Local option elections had been held for years. When I first started practicing law, candidates for office, from constable to governor, had to declare their stands on prohibition.

Prohibition was never as popular in the big cities as it was in the small towns and country areas. I really believed that it might be here to stay; I heard John Garner say as late as 1926 that it would never be repealed. Mr. Hoover, when he ran for President in 1928, called prohibition an "experiment noble in motive and far-reaching in purpose. I hope it succeeds." He never recommended a repeal of prohibition. Repeal came when Franklin D. Roosevelt was President.

Victor Berger, a Socialist who served in Congress intermittently from 1911 on, was always a controversial figure. He was refused his seat in 1918 for vigorously opposing the war. Once after the war, in a Wisconsin campaign speech, he posed the rhetorical question, "What did the United States get out of the war?" During the dramatic pause, some wag in the audience cried out, "Prohibition and the flu!" It almost broke up the meeting.

Another divisive issue during the first World War was the Woman Suffrage Amendment. During his first term, President Wilson had opposed submitting the amendment, but when he finally changed his position, he became an ardent advocate. Wilson was immensely popular in those days, and many members followed his lead.

About this time I had my first visit to the White House. Henry D. (Hal) Flood, Chairman of the Foreign Affairs Committee, invited Alben W. Barkley and me to go with him to talk with the President to make a statement declaring his position on Woman Suffrage. The President sent for a little pad and said, "Let's write a brief statement and see what it looks like on paper. I'll make a statement, but let us get it worded just right." He was not at his desk, so he sat there and wrote out his statement holding the pad on his knee, and then read it and asked for our reactions. He then authorized the committee to hand the statement to the press.

The House soon passed the resolution authorizing the submission of the amendment, but the Senate buried it in committee for about six months. Finally the President decided to address the Senate on the subject. I went to the Senate with several other members to hear the President. Applause for him was rather perfunctory. He urged adoption of the resolution as an essential war measure; most of his listeners felt it was not. He was a master of the English language, and few Americans have matched his eloquence. His performance on this occasion was not as convincing as usual Wilson speeches. He finished to mild but courteous applause.

The doors of the Senate Chamber had hardly quit swinging when John Sharp Williams, who was small of stature but powerful of mentality, addressed the Vice President. He said he loved the President, who had been very generous to him and had consulted him on many issues. "But," he continued after a dramatic pause, "when he tells me that in order to outmaneuver Hindenberg and outdistance Ludendorf it is necessary for the women of Mississippi to vote, I beg leave to most humbly disagree with him." Many people believed that in two minutes he had completely refuted the President's speech. The Senate took no action at the time. Soon after the war was over, the resolution was adopted, the states ratified it, and it became effective on August 26, 1920, as the Nineteenth Amendment.

Chapter VII

PEACE COMES

In 1918, a congressional committee of seven members was selected to visit the European war front and to investigate the operations, especially the lines of supply. The day before the committee was to sail, and after all the arrangements and reservations had been made, one of the members became ill and I was asked to take his place, so I went along. The others in the party were Alben Barkley of Kentucky, Dr. Aswell of Louisiana, Mays and Welling of Utah, Randall of California, and Linthicum of Maryland.

We sailed from New York on the *Olympic*. We traveled the entire supply line from St. Nazaire to the front, visited General Pershing's headquarters at Chaumont, and even went to the front line trenches within thirty feet of the Germans, who were right across the Eiser Canal. We traveled to the front near Verdun and the famous cathedral at Rheims near which a great battle of the war was being waged. In Nieuport, Belgium, we were pinned down for more than an hour by an artillery barrage.

We had interviews with King Albert of Belgium and Premiers Clemenceau of France and Orlando of Italy, and we were invited to dinner with the King of Italy at his chateau near the Italian front. We sent word that we had no appropriate dinner clothes, but he replied, "There is a war. Come on just as you are when you return from the battlefield." He wore a soldier's uniform and was a delightful host. The battle lines in Italy were established on opposite sides of the River Piave. We visited the Italian army, and one of our number was given the privilege of firing a cannon and sending a shell into the camp of the enemy across the river.

One of the most interesting of the men we met was Clemenceau of France. He was a rather plump man of seventy-five, who wore black gloves at his desk. He spoke beautiful English; he told us that as a young man he taught for two years in a girls' college in New England. He said that the Allies were going to win. He had fought in the Franco-Prussian War, and was anxious to recover Alsace-Lorraine from Germany. Amazingly, he called each of us by name, asked which state we were from, and talked about each of them. Welling of Utah told the Premier he was an elder in the Mormon church. The Premier then asked Mays of Utah if he was also a Mormon. Mays responded that he was not a Mormon, but "a Gentile with Mormon inclinations." Mr. Clemenceau nearly fell out of his chair with laughter. Then he said he greatly admired the loyalty and industry of the Mormon people.

On our trip we visited the combined British and American fleets, known as the Grand Fleet, just east of Edinburgh, Scotland. It stretched out for twenty miles in the nearby waters. It was continuously on the alert waiting for the German fleet to come out of a bay near Belgium. We had dinner with Admiral Rodman, Commander of the Grand Fleet, on his flagship, the battleship *New York*. He stood by as we climbed the ladder. When I reached the top of the ladder, the Admiral said, "Here! This can't be a Member of Congress. He looks like a boy." Dr. Aswell assured him I was a member. Then the Admiral insisted that I sit by his side at lunch. He said the fleet was steamed up and ready to fight at a minute's notice. The German fleet finally was engaged and destroyed by the Grand Fleet at the Battle of Jutland.

Veterans' Hospitals

In December 1918, a bill was taken up in the House to establish six veterans' hospitals over the country. A terrific fight was made over the one to be located at Dawson Springs, Kentucky. I offered a motion to strike out "Dawson Springs, Kentucky" and insert "Amarillo, Texas," changing the site of one of the hospitals. In response to the many questions this amendment precipitated, I capped my answers by stating that Potter County, of which Amarillo was the county seat, was the only county of 20,000 people in the United States that had no cemetery. One of the members asked what we did when people died. I replied that very few died in that good climate, but when they did, they were taken into the adjoining county for burial. This was literally true at that time; Amarillo was right on the boundary, and part of the city, including the only cemetery, was in Randall County. My amendment passed, but was defeated in the Senate. Some years later, with the help of the American Legion, I did secure a veterans' hospital for Amarillo.

In 1918 I was chosen as the Texas member of the Democratic National Congressional Committee, the committee responsible for electing Democratic Congressmen. In this work I made many speeches. An address I made to the Indiana Democratic Editorial Association at Evansville, Indiana, on May 30, 1918, prompted the following editorial in the *Evansville Courier*.

A RISING TEXAN

The meeting of the Indiana Editorial Association was made distinctive by the address of Hon. Marvin Jones of Texas.

The editors, accustomed to hearing at their annual meetings the most eminent men of the country, were thrilled by the eloquence of the young statesman from Texas. He began his speech late in the evening, but he got the attention of his hearers at once and held them breathlessly till his final climax was rewarded by rounds of applause.

The Lone Star state has given many eminent men to the councils of the nation. The guests in the crowded banquet hall predict that, in Congressman Jones, Texas is adding another to her luminaries.

Indiana pays her respects to Texas and congratulates her sister commonwealth on sending to the halls of congress the brilliant and eloquent young statesman, Marvin Jones. His career will be watched from the banks of the Wabash with the keenest interest and his successes with the utmost satisfaction.

Fixing Time Zones by Law

As a beginning congressman, I learned much from James R. Mann, the Republican Floor Leader. His knowledge of pending bills was fantastic. During the early part of my first term, I went to see him and asked for any suggestions he could give me. He seemed greatly pleased. He told me he had a highly competent secretary who kept a record for him of all bills favorably reported to the House. He gave me many valuable suggestions. He seemed flattered that I came to him, and after that he always took a lively interest in my career.

During the war we had had daylight saving time by national

law; nobody liked it, but in wartime they accepted it. When the war was over the Daylight Saving Act was repealed and the Interstate Commerce Commission was authorized to formulate time zones — eastern time, central time, mountain time, and Pacific time zones. The Commission ran the western boundary of the central time zone right through Oklahoma and Texas, placing the western part of each state in the mountain time. My constituents were outraged. I tried to persuade Commissioner Atchison of the ICC to return the Panhandle and South Plains to Texas time, but he would not change his position.

I drew up a bill placing the Panhandle of Oklahoma and all West Texas in the central time zone, running the dividing line along the northern Oklahoma boundary, and down the west Texas line to El Paso. Then I secured a brief hearing before the appropriate committee, which reported my measure promptly. It was late in the session, and I got the bill placed on the Unanimous Consent Calendar, which was the only chance I had to get it passed. I buttonholed everybody on the Republican side who might object, and they all agreed not to oppose it.

When my time zone bill was reached on the consent calendar, I was astonished when my old friend and mentor, James R. Mann, the Republican Floor Leader, arose and reserved the right to object. He kept me under interrogation for at least ten minutes, and I was scared to death all the time that he was going to object. I talked as fast and earnestly and persuasively as I could in answer to his questions. Finally, I said to him, "The Texas Legislature passed a resolution unanimously endorsing my bill." "Oh," he said, "that doesn't mean a thing; a legislature will pass anything." I replied, "That may be true of the Illinois Legislature, but we have a pretty good Legislature in Texas." Mr. Mann laughed and said he would not object to the passage. The bill was then passed. Soon after it had passed, Mr. Mann called me over and said, "I had no idea of objecting to your bill. You can take that record now and send it down to your folks. If it had slipped through the folks would have thought it was an easy thing to pass this bill." I realized then that he really was doing the questioning as a favor to me.

It was then the last day of the session, March 3, 1918, and I personally took the bill to Senator Sheppard. It was too late to have a Senate committee session, but the members of the committee agreed to an oral poll and a floor report. I sat by Senator Sheppard's side as he called up the bill just before midnight on March 3, 1918. It passed as the last act of that session of the Congress. The area covered thus became the only part of the United States where the time zone was fixed by law and could not be changed by the Commission.

The Armistice

The Armistice was signed on November 11, 1918, and a new era began. The transition period involving the gradual reduction of the armed services, and facing up to the problems growing out of the war and the readjustment to peacetime, meant much work for the Congress.

Chapter VIII

POSTWAR CONGRESS

IN THE ELECTION of 1918, Woodrow Wilson asked the people to return loyal Democrats to office to give him a vote of confidence. I was chosen as the Texas member of the Democratic National Congressional Committee. Billy Oldfield was chairman of that committee. On the day before the statement was made, he told me President Wilson would urge that the country elect a Democratic Congress because, with the many problems connected with the aftermath of the war and the rehabilitation, he would need loyal support in rebuilding the country. That was the burden of the President's appeal as he released it the next day. After stating his reasons for the appeal, he ended it by saying, "I submit my problems and my difficulties to you."

Many of us who knew the President planned such a statement were fearful that it might become a boomerang. Billy Oldfield felt that, with the President's great popularity, the American people would follow him. I was told that President Wilson did not want to make so strong a statement, but that he was overpersuaded by his advisors; I do not know whether this is true.

In the storm that followed the speech, the Republicans showed that they had voted for the President's war measures just as loyally as had the Democrats. When the results of the election were in, they showed 214 Democrats, 214 Republicans and 7 Progressives and Independents had been elected. In order to reelect Champ Clark as Speaker and organize the House, it was necessary for the Democrats to give the seven members, or a majority of them, good committee assignments. Thomas D. Schall of Minnesota, a Progressive, made the nominating speech for Clark as Speaker. He was a blind Member, very eloquent and an enthusiastic speech-maker.

Interesting Personalities in Congress

I spent most of my time on the floor of the House during my first term. I came to know well many of the Members of Congress in that way. I lived at Congress Hall Hotel for my first twelve years in Washington. Champ Clark and his wife and about a hundred other members lived there. It was often said facetiously that Congress never adjourned at Congress Hall. The lobby in the evening was often filled with official people who discussed their experiences and swapped stories. The hotel stood on the spot where the Longworth House Office Building is now located. It was a most distinctive hotel; one never needed to go out of the hotel, for the residents furnished their own entertainment of an evening.

Champ Clark loved to talk about American history. He could tell the key vote in each convention, both Republican and Democratic, throughout the nation's history. He knew infinite details about presidential candidates and the popular vote they received. His information on these subjects was amazing.

Clark advised me soon after I arrived in Washington to make a speech about Sam Houston. He said that if Houston had been willing to make one speech in Virginia he would have received the Virginia delegation vote in 1856 and would probably have been nominated for the presidency. He had received a number of votes in the 1848 and 1852 conventions. Houston was a native Virginian; Clark said that a delegation came from Virginia to urge that if he would make one speech to show he wanted the nomination, they could promise him Virginia's votes at the convention. Houston refused because he did not think that a man should seek that office, and he thus failed to win Virginia's support and the nomination.

Clark insisted that 1856 was a Democratic year. He considered Houston one of the five or six greatest men the United States had produced; he was popular in the South because of his fighting under Andrew Jackson and in the North because he opposed secession. Clark was convinced that Houston would have been overwhelmingly elected if he had been nominated. During his term Buchanan tried to get along with all sides, and the situation gradually deteriorated. Speaker Clark felt that, if a strong and determined man like Houston had been elected in 1856, the Civil War might have been averted, and the entire history of our country might have been altered.

Clark was also an admirer of Joseph G. (Uncle Joe) Cannon. He said that Cannon had been around so long and had seen so much of public life that you could not fool him on any public question, even if you tried. Cannon was still in the House when I was elected, and I served four years with him. Once when Uncle Joe was eighty-seven he was chosen to conduct down the center aisle a former Member of the House, Cornelius Cole, who was then one hundred years old. He had served during the Civil War. Cole made a very interesting and dramatic five-minute talk to the House. I guess Uncle Joe felt like a boy, escorting down to the well of the House a man thirteen years his senior.

One of the great old war horses of the Democratic party was W. Bourke Cockran. He was in Congress for a short time after I came. He had been keynoter at the National Democratic Convention, had served several terms in Congress, and was an orator of great persuasive powers. When the Democrats in the House were in trouble, the whip, William Oldfield, would send for him to make a speech on the floor.

One day the Democrats were about to be beaten in a close fight. Mr. Cockran was sent for and hurried to the floor; he was immediately recognized, but, unfortunately, he began speaking on the wrong side of the issue at hand. The Republicans had a gay time, laughing and cheering. Oldfield was frantic. Finally he walked up to Cockran and whispered that he was talking on the wrong side. Cockran waved him away impatiently and went on with the same speech; he talked on for about two minutes, then paused and said, "Now that is what the proponents of this measure say, but the truth is...." and then began a perfectly persuasive speech on the other side. Both sides laughed and repeatedly cheered. They cheered, I thought, not so much the quality of the speech — although he had made a good speech on both sides — as the platform cleverness of the man. Everyone had a good time.

I am not sure this speech was left in the *Record*. Many tremendously interesting speeches and parts of speeches are left out, but this incident actually occurred within the term beginning March 4, 1921. If everything were left in the record it would be much more interesting. But the custom is to submit the speech to the member who delivered it so he may correct errors. He frequently strikes out the most interesting parts, sometimes all the punch lines. Sometimes the speech is never returned, in which event it is never published.

Friends and Colleagues

John Garner, who was the head of the Texas Delegation when I entered the House, was wise in the ways of politics. He advised me to be careful of what I placed in the *Congressional Record* the first two or three years, until I had gained the confidence of my people. He told me a man is not beaten on what he does not say. A speech may sound good at the time of delivery, but a year or two later the whole picture may change. Once a Congressman has established himself as an efficient legislator, his people will trust him. Garner said he was in Congress some years before he placed a speech in the *Record*. When his remarks were submitted to him for correction of errors, he would simply pitch the copy in the waste basket. In later years his speeches appeared regularly.

Hatton Sumners looked less like a Congressman than any man in the House. And yet when he got on his feet he could make a powerful speech. He was a great student of the history, background, and philosophy of the Constitution. He strongly opposed the extension of Federal functions, and felt that vigorous democracy depended on the strength of local government. His ability as a constitutional lawyer was recognized by leading members of the American Bar Association and others throughout the nation.

He had a delightful sense of humor. Soon after I came to Congress one of my visiting constituents offered to buy me a western style hat if I would wear it. I agreed, and he bought me a good-looking cowman's hat. When I met Hatton Sumners in the hallway, he was effusive in his compliments on the hat. I began to swell up and finally said, "Yes, Hatton, it makes me look like a statesman, doesn't it?" Hatton paused, and then said, "No, I wouldn't quite say that. It goes as far as a hat can."

Sam Rayburn was one of the most level-headed men I served with during my experience in the Congress of the United States. He had abundant common sense. He was not a showy man, not a man to play to the galleries, but a man who had a way of inspiring confidence in his judgment. He took some law courses in the University of Texas while he was serving in the Legislature and I was in law school. That is where I first met him. He was elected Speaker of the House of Representatives in Texas during his second term when he was about thirty years old. He was elected to the Congress in 1912 and served for nearly fifty years. He served as Speaker longer than any other man in history. He practically spent his life in the service of the State of Texas and the Nation.

Fritz G. Lanham of Fort Worth, who came to Congress in 1919, was one of the truly able men with whom I served. His father had served many years in Congress when Fritz was a boy, so he was familiar with Washington. Fritz was one of the most beautiful speakers in the Congress and was immensely popular. He and I became fast friends and I was very fond of him. He made a great record and voluntarily retired after many years of service.

During my first term in Congress, I formed a friendship with Pat Harrison of Mississippi. He made a successful race for the Senate against James K. Vardaman, one of the twelve "wilful" men who opposed some of President Wilson's war measures. Harrison read to me his proposed opening campaign speech against Mr. Vardaman and asked for suggestions. We remained close friends during his lifetime. He was a legislator of great skill and talent and made an outstanding record. He had been a newsboy and knew the art of publicity. He tried to teach me, but I fear I was not a very apt pupil. Others among my grood friends in the House in those early years were Eugene Black and James P. Buchanan from Texas; James V. McClintic and Charles D. Carter from Oklahoma; James R. Mann of Illinois, the Republican Floor Leader; Ben Humphreys of Mississippi; and Will Bankhead of Alabama. The list is too long to include here, since I tried to become well acquainted with the entire membership during my years of early service.

The League of Nations

The story of President Wilson's journey to the Paris Peace Conference, his efforts to gain approval for the League of Nations, his second trip to Europe, his speaking tours across the nation, and his ultimate collapse, has been told many times. I think, however, that the historians are wrong about one feature of his fight over the League. They apparently assume that Henry Cabot Lodge was the man who killed the League. He led the fight and had much to do with it, but those who heard the speeches in the Senate, as I did, felt that Senator James A. Reed of Missouri delivered the fatal blow by his speech in the Senate on February 22, 1919. Up to that time, Lodge and other opponents hoped only to weaken the charter, not to defeat it.

Senator Reed's speech was an all-out, direct assault on the League. He analyzed the charter's various provisions, ridiculed their language and meaning, declared our country would have only one vote while the British empire would have six, and asserted that even small countries that had no stable government could combine and destroy us. He marshaled effectively all the standard arguments against the League and ended his speech with a ringing call to patriotism. It was one of the most eloquent appeals I have heard during my years of public service. When he had finished, Senators on both sides of the aisle stood up and cheered. I have never witnessed such a scene in the Senate. Members from both sides rushed to congratulate him. After that Senator Lodge and others began to talk of defeating the League entirely and that was, in effect, the final result.

Abolishing an Agency of Government

On January 3, 1921, there was under consideration in the House a bill which, among other things, would have made permanent the Council of National Defense, which had been established as a temporary war agency. I favored most of the bill but could see no purpose in making the agency permanent; the various defense branches were authorized to perform the Council's functions. I offered an amendment which in effect would abolish the agency.

I made what I feared was a hopeless fight, but when I finished speaking, Mr. Mann, the Republican leader, arose and made a powerful plea in support of my amendment. People from the agency urged me to withdraw the amendment, since a number of Texans were employed in the agency. I refused, and the amendment was adopted. The agency's supporters followed across and tried to save it in the Senate, but the amended bill passed the Senate on January 7, 1921. This is one of the few times an agency, once established, has been abolished. Usually they are retained and continue to grow.

An Active Member

From the beginning of my service in Congress, I took an active part in the work of the Congress, studying the various bills reported to the House and offering amendments, a number of which were adopted. At one point, I was authoring amendments with such success that one press report suggested I was becoming the "Jim Mann" of the House; Mr. Mann had by that time retired from Congress. Among the speeches I made was one on April 19, 1918, advocating a measure to provide for rehabilitating wounded soldiers; one on June 24, 1919, advocating the gradual payment of the war debt; another on September 24, 1919, advocating elimination of discriminatory freight rates against farm and ranch products; and many others, all of which are printed in the *Congressional Record.*

Chapter IX

THE 1920 ELECTION

THE ELECTION OF 1920 was a memorable one. The Democrats nominated James M. Cox for President and Franklin D. Roosevelt for Vice President. The Republican Convention featured a close contest between General Leonard Wood and Governor Frank O. Lowden. Neither was able to secure a majority. After several days, the convention named Senator Warren G. Harding for President and Calvin Coolidge as his running mate. The primary issue of the campaign was whether the proposed League of Nations should be ratified by the United States Senate. The Republicans won by a wide margin. A New York *Times*' editorial later declared that the splendid idealism of Woodrow Wilson had gone down in a crash of materialism.

The Republicans made a clean sweep. Only 131 Democrats were all that were left in the House to hold the party together, and 121 of these were from the South or border states. Republicans were elected from many districts that had always been considered safely Democratic. Speaker Champ Clark was defeated by a man named T. W. Hukriede. Republicans were so numerous in the House that there was not sufficient seating capacity on their side of the aisle, and they spilled over to the Democratic side.

Some unusual people were elected. Many of them served only one term. One of them, William O. Atkeson, was from Missouri; he attended all sessions but never said anything. He was an interesting looking man. After several months I found occasion to engage him in friendly conversation. He said his district had always been Democratic, no one had wanted the Republican nomination, five others before him had declined to run, and he agreed to run to help hold the party together, with no thought of winning. He knew he did not belong in the House, and there was no chance of re-election, but he was saving his money and learning all he could. He was sixty-six years old and appreciated the honor that had come to his family by his election. I was impressed by his candor and common sense, and urged him to take an active part in House affairs, but he preferred to just sit it out and try to vote intelligently.

Another new Congressman was Manuel Herrick, a rather strange man from Oklahoma, whose election many regarded as a political accident. His district had been represented for many years by the distinguished Dick T. Morgan, who was very popular and was considered unbeatable. Before the primary, but after it was too late for anyone else to file, Dick Morgan died following a serious operation. Various Republicans tried to persuade Herrick to withdraw and let the local committee name the party candidate, but he refused. The Republican National Committee was fearful that the House would be almost equally divided between the two major parties, and advised local Republicans to support Herrick. He was elected in the national Republican landslide.

Herrick announced for Speaker before he reached Washington. As it turned out, his vote was not needed in the Republican organization. He pulled some laughable stunts and repeatedly embarrassed his party. Naturally, he was encouraged in his shenanigans by the Democrats. He claimed that he had developed copper-faced Hereford cattle, a breed that most livestock people knew nothing about. He missed the first Congressional reception at one of the embassies because he had no dress clothes, but for the next one he rented a tuxedo in a shop on F Street and was determined to attend. A few thoughtful friends took up a collection to bribe a taxi driver to get lost in Rock Creek Park and other places, and never find the embassy. Finally the taxi driver took him home, apologizing for his inability to find the place, and refusing to make any charge.

Herrick finally made it to the British Embassy. He walked to the punchbowl, grabbed the ladle and drank two helpings from that dipper, grabbed two handfuls of sandwiches and ate them, then took a highly polished apple from the fruit decorations and ate it as he walked among the other guests. He complimented a distinguished-looking sentinel standing at the entrance to the reception room in a decorated uniform by saying "You shore did give us a fine feed." The Englishman continued to stare into space, without batting an eyelash.

Champ Clark and History

To me one of the great tragedies of the 1920 election was the defeat of Speaker Champ Clark of Missouri. He knew more about political history of the United States than any other man I have ever known. He felt that he would have been President of the United States had not William Jennings Bryan of Nebraska deserted him at the Baltimore convention in 1912.

That convention gave Champ Clark a majority of the votes, but he did not receive the necessary two-thirds vote required at that time. When the New York delegation announced that it wanted to switch and cast its votes for Champ Clark, Bryan arose and withdrew his support from Clark, notwithstanding the fact that his delegation had been instructed to support Clark for the nomination. In a fiery speech, Bryan denounced the Tammany delegation and declared that he would not support a Wall Street candidate. This threw the convention into an uproar, which was finally resolved by the nomination of Woodrow Wilson on the 46th ballot.

Clark was greatly disappointed, since he realized that at his age that was probably his last chance to be elected President. He continued, however, as Speaker of the House and remained immensely popular with his colleagues. He took a personal interest in all the members of the House; I found his advice and counsel very helpful. The Speaker pointed out that while a member was working on one committee, the other forty committees of the House were also grinding away at the many thousands of bills introduced. No member can stay well informed on all matters upon which he must pass. Congressmen thus become interdependent, each relying on the specialties of others for information about and understanding of the issues for which he must answer to his constituents.

Champ Clark was a great reader and student of history. He could talk at great length about Napoleon. Once in later years when I undertook to check on one of Mr. Clark's stories about Napoleon, I ran into a statement that Napoleon once pointed to the map of China and said, "There lies China, a sleeping giant. Let him sleep; the nation that awakens him will be sorry." Further research disclosed substantially the same story in three other histories of Napoleon. Two of the other histories varied the last sentence: "Let him sleep, for when he awakens he will move the world." It seems prophetic that Napoleon should have made that statement more than 150 years ago; the sleeping giant apparently is now awakening.

Speaker Clark also had an interesting version of the story of the duel between General Andrew Jackson and Major Dickson, which arose over some remark the Major had made about General Jackson's wife, Rachel. Major Dickson was an expert pistol shot, and General Jackson was not. Jackson decided he would wait until Dickson had fired and hoped to survive to shoot second. Jackson was very slender. He practically always wore a long loose coat, which he did on this occasion.

Major Dickson fired his pistol but Jackson did not fall. Jackson then took deliberate aim and pulled the trigger, but the pistol snapped; he cocked the pistol again and fired and killed Major Dickson. Jackson's aide noticed blood on Jackson's coat. It seemed that Jackson had twisted his body within the loose coat. Major Dickson probably hit the spot he aimed for, but the bullet had not inflicted a fatal injury. General Jackson never fully recovered from that wound. His enemies and the friends of Major Dickson claimed he had no right after his pistol snapped to have what amounted to a second shot.

Blue Discharge for Minors

In September 1921, the House was considering the Army bill, H.R. 15943. For years it had been the custom of the Army to give a "blue discharge" to any minor who had enlisted without the consent of his parents and who had represented himself as being of legal age. A blue discharge was less than honorable. It handicapped the young man later on in many ways. I offered an amendment to require the Army to issue an honorable discharge in such cases. The amendment was adopted and became part of the Army bill which passed February 8, 1921.

Chapter X

OF MANY THINGS

It was a custom prior to 1925 to allow each congressional district one new post office building whenever a building program was scheduled, which was usually every four years. A district that had a large city or two would get a building costing considerably more than a district that only had small cities, and some districts would get a building that was not truly needed.

I had a district of fifty-three counties with a rapidly growing population. In 1920, I wrote a letter to Andrew Mellon, Secretary of the Treasury, telling him I thought this was a mistaken policy. I pointed out that under this policy one district might get a post office that was not needed, while some other district might have several towns that needed a post office, but only one could be constructed.

I suggested that this old logrolling practice be abandoned and that the problem be approached on a businesslike basis. My plan was that any city in the nation should receive a post office when the postal receipts of the office reached and maintained a minimum amount for a three-year period, so that it would be good business for the government to have its own building in that locality.

The Secretary responded, complimenting the suggestion, indicating that such a policy might prove to be too expensive at that time, and promising to study the matter further. I heard nothing further about it and did nothing more; my party was in the minority, and I thought there was little chance for the adoption of my suggestion. Years later a newspaper reporter asked me what kind of a letter I had written Secretary Mellon. Mellon in an interview that day had told of my letter and said he liked the plan and intended gradually to put it into operation.

Some years later a general Post Office building bill carried appropriations for post office buildings in six growing towns in my district; the six cost no more than some individual post office buildings in the larger cities. I was advised in advance, but was asked to give no publicity until the announcement date for the program. The rule then became effective that no post office would be recommended for construction in any city until minimum receipts should be reached and maintained for a period of about three years. I think this was a wise change of policy, and I am happy to have had a small part in its adoption.

Texas Tech University

I attended the Democratic State Convention in Fort Worth in the summer of 1920. Pat Neff of Waco had just been nominated for governor. The West Texas Chamber of Commerce and various other West Texas business organizations sought the convention's endorsement of a resolution calling for the establishment of a technical state college on the high plains. I was asked to lead the fight.

It was the one big fight of the convention. In closing the argument for the resolution, I noted the vast areas of West Texas, the greatly increasing population, the farming and livestock raising, and the industrial development of that great area. I emphasized that much of that area was more than six hundred miles from the University at Austin and more than seven hundred from Texas A&M at College Station. I pointed out that West Texas students attending those schools had to change trains two or three times, and that Amarillo, Lubbock and other growing West Texas cities were nearer to the capitals of Oklahoma, Kansas, Colorado and New Mexico than to Austin. I also stated that the area I represented was twenty percent larger than the State of Ohio, and larger than any state east of the Mississippi river, except Georgia, and that it was only a part of the area that would be served by the proposed new school.

Many news reporters, including Silliman Evans of the Fort Worth *Star-Telegram*, thought the resolution would carry, but it was defeated by about twenty votes out of several hundred delegates. At the next session of the Legislature, Senator W. H. Bledsoe introduced a measure to establish Texas Technological College at Lubbock, the measure was enacted, and Governor Neff signed it promptly.

Helium

Helium is a distinct element that is sometimes found in natural gas and in certain minerals and mineral waters. It was first discovered in the spectrum of the sun by astronomers in 1868; its name is derived from the Greek word *helios,* meaning the sun. It is an inert, non-combustible gas that has 92 percent of the lifting power of hydrogen. Since it is not flammable, it is much preferred over hydrogen for use in balloons. Incendiary bullets would immediately set fire to a balloon filled with hydrogen, but not to one filled with helium.

When it was first extracted it was a chemical curiosity costing about $1,500 per cubic foot. It is separated from natural gas by a process of liquefaction. The first real development of helium extraction came from the research of Dr. C. W. Seibel and other scientists during World War I. The first plant was established at Petrolia, Texas, and the next at Fort Worth. Soon after the war, the largest known gas field in the world was discovered in the Panhandle of Texas. I had a test sample of the gas sent to an old classmate named Richey in the Bureau of Mines. It developed that much of the gas had a higher helium content than had been found in any other gases thus far discovered.

My old friend Fritz G. Lanham and I had a tussle over the location of a new helium plant; he wanted it three hundred miles away in Fort Worth, and I wanted it in the Panhandle. The Bureau of Mines people told me that, if I would help them secure the purchase of the gas rights in one complete gas reservoir, they would locate the new plant near the field at Soncy in the Panhandle. I helped secure 50,000 acres of gas lands, 13,000 acres purchased by deed, and gas and mineral rights acquired on the remaining 37,000 acres. When this was accomplished I received a wire from President Coolidge announcing a modern $3,000,000 helium plant at Soncy. Dr. Seibel, one of the pioneers in the development program, was placed in charge of the Panhandle plant and served there for many years. A contract was made with a large gas pipeline company to use the gas after the helium had been extracted and thus conserve all the helium in the reservoir. For years this installation remained the only operating helium plant in the world. Later, however, helium-bearing gases were found and developed in other areas.

After World War I, Ferdinand von Zeppelin of Germany developed large air passenger transport vehicles filled with hydrogen. His Graf-Zeppelin carried many passengers and flew around the world in 1929, landing in Lakehurst, New Jersey, and in Los Angeles. One of the largest he later built was the "Hindenberg No. 1," which burned at Lakehurst, where thirty-five of the ninety-seven passengers and crew members died in the flames.

Herr von Zeppelin later sought to secure enough helium from this country to fill two airships of the Zeppelin type. I attended the hearing when he appeared before a congressional committee. He gave assurance that he did not want to use the helium for military purposes and he made a fine impression as a sincere and honest man. But Hitler by that time had come into power. Harold Ickes, Secretary of the Interior, strongly opposed letting any amount be sold for shipment abroad. After the hearings, Congress passed an act forbidding the exportation of helium.

Bolshevism

Soon after the end of World War I, a movement began which advocated the overthrow of our government by force. News accounts reported speeches openly advocating the use of the bomb and the torch to achieve social and political reform. I made a speech on the floor of the House on October 27, 1919, which caused much favorable comment. I deplored the radical and revolutionary doctrines being bruited abroad in the country as unpatriotic, un-American and undesirable. While I favored freedom of speech and thought, I suggested that those who preached violent revolution in preference to persuasive methods did not deserve to be left in a country that had grown great and powerful in recognition of law and constitutional rights. Whether citizens or aliens, they might be deported to live together on remote islands, trying out their absurd doctrines on one another. Newspaper reports of this speech referred to me as "one of the coming big men in Congress."

Freight Rate Discrimination

The Democrats were in the minority in the House for ten years to the day from March 4, 1921, so most of the major legislation bore the names of the Republican chairmen. I continued to be active, however, and was successful in adding a number of amendments to pending legislation. Also, I helped to shape legislation in the Agriculture Committee.

In the early 1920's, I began the long fight to remove freight rate discrimination against farm commodities, especially those destined for export. Exportation of manufactured articles had for many years been encouraged by freight rate reduction from the point of manufacture to the point of embarkation. For example, if two plows were shipped from Moline, Illinois, to New Orleans and unloaded at the same place, one for sale in Louisiana, the other for foreign shipment, the freight rate on the latter would be only half as much. This rate differential was as justifiable for farm commodities as it was for manufactured goods. I continued this fight through the years; I shall refer to it later.

Shortage of Railway Cars

In 1919, the Texas Panhandle and South Plains produced their biggest wheat crop in history. There was a shortage of railway cars throughout the country. About 7,000,000 bushels of wheat were threshed and piled on the ground; the elevators were full. It was difficult to convince the Interstate Commerce Commission that an emergency existed; they evidently thought I was exaggerating.

After I made a speech on the floor of the House, the Commission at last said they would send a man to investigate. I told them to send a good one and I would go with him. They sent J. W. Mulhern, an experienced investigator; we went all over the region and saw several million bushels of wheat, threshed and piled on the ground. Mr. Mulhern said he believed I had underestimated the emergency. He wired Washington that there would be great losses if a blowing rain should come.

The Commission named Assistant Director General Bryce Clagett to work out a comprehensive plan for relieving the freight congestion and moving the wheat crop. The cars soon came rolling in and the situation was relieved. Uncle Joe Cannon said somewhat facetiously on the floor that he went down to the Commission to ask for some cars for his area and was told they had all been sent to the Panhandle of Texas. In his speech, he referred to me as "one of the ablest and most effective of the younger members of the House." So high a compliment from such a man was greatly appreciated.

New Railway Construction

I also made a fight on two features of the Esch Act of 1919. One feature gave the Interstate Commerce Commission the right to determine where and whether any new railroad extension should be constructed. This provision would make it difficult to secure new railway construction in a rapidly growing area. My amendment to eliminate this provision was defeated. The main argument against my amendment was that it directed the Commission to establish rates guaranteeing the railways 6 percent net profit, and that construction in sparsely settled areas might force higher rates. I asked them wryly why they did not just require pioneers in new areas to use wheelbarrows, so as to protect already satisfied areas.

I also fought to eliminate the provision which authorized the Commission to direct the allocation of freight cars. I felt the railroads were in a much better position to handle this than any agency, no matter how competent. In order to defeat my amendment, the Chairman made a strong plea not to load the bill down. Even so, it was defeated by only a small margin.

There is no doubt that the Commission had done valuable work from the beginning. In fact, the first such commission was the Texas Railroad Commission, planned by John H. Reagan who was its first chairman, and who had been a member of the Confederate Cabinet. That commission became the pattern for the Interstate Commerce Commission. Broad powers of regulation were essential since the railroads practically had a monopoly of freight and passenger transportation. But by the 1920's the whole picture had changed. The horseless carriage had come along and gradually developed into a new form of transportation.

It is often said that Henry Ford invented mass production; what he really invented was mass distribution. Theretofore when anyone gained a practical control of any market, the prices were raised. But Mr. Ford reversed this process: he reduced prices to encourage wider use, and he practically gained control of the low-priced car market. It was said frequently that he put the nation on wheels.

Buses and trucks, and later airplanes, entered the field in passenger and freight service. Open competition largely regulates the rates. But the broad powers of regulation of the railroads by the Commission, once so essential, have in some instances become a decided handicap to railway transportation. When the railroads want to reduce rates even temporarily, their competitors usually demand a hearing, and this suspends the new rate until the hearings are had and the Commission finally determines the matter.

Some critics argue that the Commission should be limited to preventing discriminatory rates and rebates, leaving ratemaking largely to competition. The Commission's powers should at least be modified so that it could make rates immediately effective, and that contests should not be permitted to hold up effective rates during emergencies.

Chapter XI

SIDELIGHTS

One of my favorites as a public speaker was blind Senator Thomas P. Gore of Oklahoma, one of the most eloquent speakers I heard during my long experience in public life. In Oklahoma, one had only to announce that Thomas Gore was going to speak, and a crowd would come to hear him.

He was opposed on one occasion by a man named Bell, who was unable to draw a crowd. Bell tried following Senator Gore, but the crowd would melt away. He than began speaking before Senator Gore spoke. One day when a platform had been erected for Senator Gore, Bell's friends placed a truck right across the street and Bell began speaking a short time before Gore was booked to speak, and continued into the time allotted to Senator Gore. Finally, Senator Gore walked up onto his platform and simply faced across the street at his adversary, and waited for Bell to finish. Then when all was quiet, said, "Methinks I hear the tinkling of a far-away tiny bell." It brought down the house, and thereafter Bell ceased to interfere with Senator Gore's audiences.

Senator Gore became blind at 15 years of age when a cigar lighter exploded in his face. He was one of the Senators who, just prior to World War I, were branded by Woodrow Wilson as the "Wilful Twelve, who represented nobody but themselves." In April 1917 Senator Gore also voted against the war resolution.

Scott Ferris, a Member of the House from Oklahoma, defeated Senator Gore in the Democratic primary in 1918. I passed through Oklahoma City about ten days before the election on a night when Senator Gore was speaking. The crowd at first was noisy, restless and hostile, but he soon had them cheering wildly. I have always felt that if Gore had had time to cover the entire State he would have won renomination. His friends were so disappointed that they helped the Republicans defeat Scott Ferris in the general election, although it was generally a Democratic year.

After the war Senator Gore was reelected to the Senate and remained there until his death. His wife and his grandson, Gore Vidal, often read to him. Highway 66 became a continuous good highway from Chicago to Los Angeles, passing through Claremore, Oklahoma, the home of Will Rogers. A banquet was held at the Mayflower Hotel in Washington seeking to have the highway named for Will Rogers. Most of these speeches ran to a pattern and there was much repetition. Finally, the toastmaster called on Senator Gore; I thought for once he would be stumped, but he again stole the entire show. In essence he said,

In a real sense if Will Rogers were to be properly honored the tribute should not start in Chicago but should have its beginning in primordial chaos; and it should carry through all life and human activity and end not in California but beyond the sunset. He belonged not to our time but to the ages. No tribute therefore would be adequate that did not include all the States, all time and all human activities.

I wish I might have had a copy of his speech. When the meeting adjourned I told him I thought his speech the most eloquent I had ever heard; without a moment's hesitation, he replied, "Praise from Cicero himself is praise indeed." As usual, he had come up with a reply to me that defied any further comment.

Sectional v. National Control

On January 8, 1921, the Chairman of the House Appropriations Committee, Congressman Madden of Illinois, evidently elated by the overwhelming sweep of his party in the House of Representatives, issued an amazing press release. He said that for the first time in history the territory north of the Ohio and east of the Mississippi rivers (an area less than a fourth of the nation) would have a majority in the House of Representatives; that this section paid more than 84 per cent of the taxes collected by the government and that the Republicans from the tax-paying belt were properly in complete control. It was further asserted that under Democratic Administrations the South had been in the saddle.

I read a statement into the record the same day, saying it would be a sad day when money alone is the criterion for control of the government. I declared that every citizen, rich or poor, should have an equal voice in the affairs of the nation. In no other way could free government be maintained. I stated that I regretted to see sectionalism again raise its ugly head. I suggested that many of the securities held in the section to which Mr. Madden referred were based upon physical properties in the South and West. I noted that this was the first time in all the glorious history of this country a Representative in Congress had intimated that patriotism, love of country, brains or ability were to be gauged by the meanderings of the Ohio or the sluggish flow of the Mississippi.

Many members asked for copies of my address. Naturally Congressman Madden's statement was unpopular in the South and West; indeed, most Members from the East thought the statement an unfortunate mistake.

Packer Legislation

In the early part of 1921, the Agriculture Committee began extensive hearings on proposed legislation to regulate the packers and stockyards. It was a far-ranging proposal. Before that time the so-called "Big Packers" had owned and controlled the stockyards in the terminal cities and determined which buyers should be permitted to use the stockyards. The measure required the packers and processors to dispose of their interests in the stockyards. The bill also gave the Secretary of Agriculture broad powers of regulation.

Representatives of livestock growers and farm organizations testified to the effect that the packers were in collusion and that the market was thus controlled. Naturally, the packers denied all these charges. The hearings lasted nearly a month. The presidents of the companies, Phil Armour, Louis Swift, Tom Wilson, Cudahay, and many others, attended much of the time. The issues were hard fought on both sides. It developed that Thomas Wilson of Wilson & Company was especially well informed on the various issues. Mr. Wilson had started boys' and girls' farm clubs, an idea that later developed into 4-H Clubs, which have done so much for rural America. Finally Kentucky's Dave Kincheloe of the Committee on Agriculture invited him to speak off the record. Among other things Mr. Wilson said, in substance:

I have been in this business since I was eighteen years old, punching the cattle through the chutes with a stick with a nail in the end for $1.00 a day. I know you gentlemen are going to pass some legislation. Perhaps you should do so. In this business some practices may have developed that need correction. I have but one request to make. I am sure you gentlemen don't want to destroy the packers. The packers are distinctively American institutions. They are a vital part of our great livestock marketing system. Correct the evils you find, but leave us otherwise free to perform our useful and necessary marketing functions. More than 80 cents out of every dollar that the packers ultimately collect is paid to the grower of the livestock. I challenge comparison on that score with any other marketing process. We will accept whatever restrictions you may write into law. You have been generous in hearing our testimony, and we now must rely on your good judgment in writing the final provisions of the law.

I believe we were all sorry at the end that Mr. Wilson's talk was not taken down along with the other testimony. We were all impressed with his sincerity and candor. The Packers and Stockyards Act, passed later that year, divorced the ownership of the stockyards from the packinghouses and conferred many regulatory powers on the Secretary of Agriculture, but provided for court review of the reasonableness of any orders issued. The act worked well and, with amendments from time to time, is still in effect.

Other Activities

Although our party was in the minority, I remained active during the early twenties. I introduced bills, attended committee meetings, offered amendments and made speeches in the House. I spoke on the tariff, on the question of furnishing arms and ammunition to other countries, and on Henry Ford's offer to lease and operate Muscle Shoals. Most of the solutions to these and other problems came in later days and times, and discussion of them in the context of the 1920's would be of little interest to today's reader.

There were three subjects in which I was vitally interested and which are of continuing vital importance. First, I offered bills and amendments during the 1920's looking toward research into new uses, new manufactures, and new markets for agricultural commodities; second, I worked on a system of farm credits that would reduce the high interest rates paid by farmers and livestock producers and which seriously handicapped their economy; and third, I did all I could to emphasize the importance of soil conservation to every man, woman and child in America. I had these issues in my platform when I made the first race for the Congress.

Chapter XII

THE HARDING ADMINISTRATION

THE HARDING ADMINISTRATION was almost overwhelmed with its own top-heavy majority. At first blush one would think this would be a great advantage. But our government, our businesses, our farms, our livestock producing, our manufacturing, our marketing, and even our social life are based upon free and open competition. As a monopoly situation develops, participants tend to grow careless and wasteful as to quality and service. This principle applies especially in our two-party system; when one party gets a large majority it is difficult to keep the members working together. That is just what happened during the Harding administration.

Harding was inaugurated March 4, 1921. There was no regular session of the Congress until December, and he called no special session. The new President was easygoing. He made no drive for new legislation, even though one of the main slogans of his campaign was the need for a change. There was much news about the President's golf, his yachting, and his dog, "Laddie Boy." Will Rogers was booked for a week at Keith's vaudeville theatre in downtown Washington. While twisting his rope he pulled this gem: "I came to Washington Thursday to see the new President. The appointment clerk told me the President goes yachting every Thursday and doesn't get back until Tuesday. I told him I will be here a week, so I can see him Wednesday, but the clerk told me he plays golf on Wednesday. The next time I vote for a President, I'm going to vote for a seasick man with a wooden leg. But I'll admit that 'Laddie Boy' has had more publicity in eight months than the Democrats were able to get in eight years."

The skit was not repeated after the second night, on request from the White House. Someone who heard Rogers the next week in Baltimore reported Rogers as saying he thought everyone understood his Washington skit was intended as sheer fun and entertainment and he was sorry if anyone took it seriously. Rogers was quoted as saying that he had said much worse things about President Wilson but that Wilson had laughed as heartily as anyone.

The Word "Tariff"

In the early part of the Harding administration a bill providing for a very high tariff came up for discussion in the House. In the course of this discussion I made a speech in which I told the history of the word "tariff." Since that part of my speech attracted a great deal of comment, I quote it here:

Mr. JONES of Texas. Mr. Chairman, in the early part of the eighth century a band of marauders under a leader by the name of Tarif crossed the straits from Africa and landed on the southern shores of Spain. His band was held together by the spoils of conquest. The horde consisted of Moors, Berbers, Syrians, Africans, and a few Arabs, all bent on plunder. They were Mohammedans, and were in a sense the vanguard of the followers of Islam in their westward swing but cared less for their religion than for booty. Tarif plundered the country and established a little seaport town, Tarifa, which, with its old moorish walls, to this day perpetuates the name and memory of the leader of this motley aggregation of robbers and conquerors. Tarif, later reinforced by his superior, Tarik, and his chief, Musa, overran a great deal of Spain. This baron lived in a chateau that was feudal in its magnificence, and in plundering fashion levied certain duties on all commerce that came through or approached the town of Tarifa. He made the people who toiled pay tribute to him as a sort of robber ruler. The gleaming sword was his collecting agency, and he would hold up ship and caravan in piratical fashion and make them pay tribute to sustain his conquest and luxury. From that town Tarifa, which was named after the princely Tarif, the English word 'tariff' is taken. The name arose in heathenism. It meant forced contribution of the many to the few. How fitting that a policy which finds its consummation in this bill should have had such an origin.

The bill was passed in 1922; it came to be known as the Fordney-McCumber Tariff Act (H.R. 74456). The Democratic National Committee included the above quotation in the handbook for speakers during the campaign of 1924.

The Scandals and Politics

I was never convinced that President Harding did anything improper. I think he was simply the victim of men he trusted. He could not escape criticism for choosing corrupt officials. As matters grew worse, an investigating committee was appointed, led by Senator Thomas J. Walsh of Montana. The Teapot Dome oil and other scandals were brought to light.

After President Harding's death in 1923, Vice President Calvin Coolidge became President. Many people thought the Democrats would surely win in 1924 because of the scandals. But William G. McAdoo of California and Al Smith of New York got into a bitter fight for the nomination at the convention in New York. There were also several other candidates, including Senator Oscar W. Underwood of Alabama and Governor Albert C. Ritchie of Maryland.

I attended that stormy convention. Franklin D. Roosevelt made his "Happy Warrior" nominating speech for Al Smith after which about two thousand Smith boosters crashed the convention with numerous banners and brass bands; the din was terrific. The Chairman was helpless; he could as easily have dammed the Mississippi with toothpicks as he could have evicted those who broke in. The Smith crowd appeared to have control of the convention, but the opposing forces were well organized; the lines held, and no one could get a majority. More than 100 roll calls were taken, going on monotonously for several days. People were saying that if the Democrats couldn't even run a convention, they surely couldn't run the government.

Many people thought the Democrats lost the election at that convention. They finally compromised by nominating John W. Davis, an outstanding New York lawyer and former Member of Congress, for President, and Charles Bryan, a brother of William J. Bryan, of Nebraska, for Vice President. A strong campaign was waged by the Democrats, but somehow they could not overcome the effect of the prolonged convention. I made a speech comparing the Republican party to a circus — calling it the Republican street parade and GOP circus. The Democratic National Committee had many thousands of copies of the speech reprinted and sent out in the campaign. Since it is not very long and attracted so much attention, it is set out here:

THE REPUBLICAN STREET PARADE AND THE G.O.P. CIRCUS
Speech of Congressman Marvin Jones in the House of Representatives
April 1, 1924

Mr. JONES. Mr. Chairman, during my boyhood days I loved the circus. I would do anything from driving tent stakes to carrying water for the elephants in order to secure the privilege of admission. For weeks before the arrival I would read every circular and every ad which described with graphic detail all of the dare-devil performances, the tight-rope walker, the clowns, and the wonderful trained animals. Day after day and time after time these circulars, with all their lurid language, would be diligently sought, eagerly read, and carefully preserved. As the time approached the circulars became larger, the language more lurid, and the excitement more intense. Always the circus was preceded by a street parade. Always the circus was claimed to be the world's greatest show. The elephants were the biggest, the tents were the largest, the wild animals were the wildest, the rhinoceros the most terrible, and the clowns the most clownish in all the tides of time. But in spite of those old-time ads and the rare old circus days I want to call your attention to what is beyond question the greatest of all displays; greater than Hagenback, greater than Barnum, greater than Ringling, greater even than Mollie Bailey, greater than all combined. Gentlemen, allow me to call your attention to the Republican street parade and the G.O.P. circus.

Nothing like it in the history of the world; no such parade, no such animals, no such humbugs since the morning stars sang together. In the first cage, furnished in mahogany, swimming in oil, and drawn by six or eight cows, is Albert B. Fall, the Interior decorator. Without hesitation we pronounce him the highest-priced Interior decorator in captivity. Will positively appear in every performance, with all his constitutional privileges intact. This alone will be worth the price of admission. In the second cage will be Harry Asbestos Daugherty — Asbestos, because he is hard to fire — the political Houdini, also the political hoodoo. To quote — with apologies to Fritz Lanham — from the famous Hamburg show, "There are some who do not believe in the hoodoo, and there are others who do." This is positively the only specimen in the whole wide world who can sit on the lid when the teapot is boiling, when the lid is red hot, and when the pressure is 5,000 pounds per square inch. This rare animal of the Cabinet type will positively appear in the main show in a blood-curdling act in three invisible rings at once, known as, "Now he resigns and now he does not," with Roxie Stinson as ringmaster. Do not miss the main performance. (Laughter)

In the next vehicle, ladies and gentlemen, is a rare fowl of the bantam type in a miniature cage, Brigadier General Sawyer. He measures 3 feet from the crown of his head to the soles of his shoes, and 3 feet from the soles of his shoes to the crown of his head, making a grand total of 6 feet. Do not fail to bring your opera glasses and see this feature. He will demonstrate the artistic and painless method of operating on the United States Treasury for $6,000 per year without a struggle. The next cage, flecked with burnished gold and costing $1,000 per fleck, also carrying a teapot for a radiator, will contain the rare type of the genus homo, commonly known as Harry Sinclair. Wherever he goes he carries a satchel, and during the main performance will deliver a lecture on the wonders of Europe during troublous times in America. He will also deliver a eulogy upon the acrobatic proclivities of two of his erstwhile pets.

In the next cage will be found two rare specimens, both of whom are descendants of an illustrious ancestor, and who will do a double pantomime. One of them will read a strictly modernized version of —

> The boy stood on the burning deck,
> Whence all but him had fled;
> But the flames becoming furious,
> He also up and fled.

The other will wear a messenger cap and uniform and will continually engage in the delightful pastime of carrying important messages dipped in crude, at the same time guaranteeing to know nothing as to what they contain.

Next in line will be the G.O.P. elephant, somewhat "Wrigley" perhaps, but still able to quiet his nerves, having learned for that purpose the gentle art of chewing gum and having the bruised places massaged with oil. Accompanying the elephant will be the Republicans — regulars, progressives, and mavericks. The regulars will ride the Republican elephant all the time, regardless of which way he is going. The progressives will ride a part of the time and try to lead the balky beast the remaining portion of the time, sometimes giving the animal a vicious kick, but always holding onto the tail as evidence of their party allegiance. The mavericks, being unbranded, help lead when it is popular and will ride the old animal when it is profitable.

The regulars will announce that they believe it is always better to be regular than right.

The progressives will announce that they think it is sometimes better to be right than regular.

The mavericks will announce that they think it is always better to be expedient.

I may add on the whole, my sympathies are with the progressives. I include such hair-raising features as the Kansas delegation in a mad foot race to the telegraph station — and by the way, I may add that I think that race was for a very laudable purpose. Also, Nicholas, the lion tamer; Begg, the auctioneer; Lasker, the shipbuilder; and Means, the doughboy. LaGuardia will loop the loop. Hill will sell the pink lemonade; Ned McLean will write an editorial in code on "Locating as a matter of principle the elusive Slemp in the social Everglades of Florida — after the curfew has rung." Will Hays will handle the motion-picture rights; Frear will collect the excess profits, and Madden will appropriate the money. The whole layout will bear the inscription "The only party that's fit to rule." (Laughter).

The feature performance will be Kareful Kal, the only politician in captivity who has ever been able to hold office for 25 years and always have himself photographed milking a cow or pitching hay when notified of his nomination, and to do it at no other time — thus qualifying both as a magician and a tight-rope walker. This artist from the realm of make-believe, accompanied by the White House cat, will walk an imaginary tight wire while endeavoring to uphold the law in one hand and Harry Daugherty in the other. At the same time, he will undertake to flirt with Wall Street with one eye and fool the farmers of the Northwest with the other. He guarantees to chew gum through the entire performance.

It is claimed that this is the only show in the world carrying nothing but clowns. More details will be furnished later, but in the meantime —

> "Don't fool with the animals —
> Don't slip in the oil, and
> Don't miss the main show."

say sympathy, because they are entirely too good to be Republicans, and not quite good enough to be Democrats.

Following will come the calliope, or steam piano with our somewhat corpulent, but not altogether unsymmetrical, friend from Kansas as the stellar performer — typical of the prairies and their broad expanse — and trying desperately to drown out the discord prevailing in the other parts of the parade.

Do not miss the parade, which will take place at 10 a.m. on the 32nd day of July, rain or shine.

Two performances daily.

Secretary Hughes will feed the animals.

Time will forbid a description of the main performance of this political menagerie de luxe. But it will be the grandest, most gorgeous, and most spectacular performance in the history of humbuggery, and will

Positively the farewell tour and final performance of the Republican Street Parade and the G.O.P. Circus.

Keeping Cool with Coolidge

During the 1924 campaign a picture was taken of President Coolidge pitching hay; it was published all over the country. I made a speech noting that the President had on a pair of unionalls drawn over a pair of dress trousers, the latter showing clearly in the opening around the waist; that he had on a white shirt with cuffs; that he had no hat, and in spite of the summer sun his hair was perfectly combed; and that there was no hay around except that on his pitchfork. I declared that anyone who had ever seen the corner of a hay meadow would recognize the photograph as a campaign pose. Coolidge paid no attention to my charges. After the election Alben Barkley undertook to get a rise out of him. The newspapers carried an account of the President's installing a wooden hobby horse in the White House for exercise. Barkley took the floor to rib him about the wooden horse. Finally, one of the Members interrupted Barkley to inquire, "What's wrong with that? How is the President going to get any exercise? Do you want him to walk?" Barkley replied, "I'm willing to give him his walking papers any time."

A strenuous campaign was waged by the Democrats, but somehow they never seemed able to overcome the public's reaction to the monotonous roll calls at the convention. But more important to the Republican victory was the personality of Calvin Coolidge, his New England thrift, his posture of economy in government after the heavy expenditures of the World War, and the fact that his name was in no way connected with the oil scandals. Coolidge was elected by a substantial margin.

During his entire elective term, President Coolidge preached economy and practiced it in private and public life. Many stories were told of his ability to economize in words as well as otherwise. The story is told of a woman dinner companion who told the President of her wager with a friend that she could get him to say three words during the banquet. The President responded, "You lose." On another occasion a book by a noted iconoclast sought by insinuations of personal misconduct to tear down the reputation of George Washington. When a newsman asked Coolidge what he thought of the book, Coolidge commented, "I see the Washington monument is still standing."

Congressman Fred Purnell of Indiana told me of the experience he and four of his friends had during a courtesy call on the President. The President unlocked his desk using a large bunch of keys, took five cigars out of a box and handed each a cigar, and locked the box back in the desk drawer. When another friend came in, Coolidge again unlocked the desk and handed the new man a cigar. A little later one of the visitors, thinking he might get an extra cigar, told the President his seven-year-old boy would be thrilled to have the band off the President's cigar. Mr. Coolidge again unlocked the desk, took the band off a cigar, handed the guest the band, placed the cigar back in the box, and relocked the drawer. Many of these acts of economy were deliberate. People would say, "If he is that careful in his own affairs, he won't waste public funds."

Coolidge was not a bad President. The country continued to grow and prosper. He had a sort of mystic faith in the quality of business planning. Indeed much credit is due the most fabulous business system in the history of the world. But Coolidge may have gone to extremes. Allowing big business to go completely unregulated is like turning a fire engine loose without a governor. Those who think big business is bad and should be handcuffed and hobbled are even worse. The wiser policy would seem to be a middle course.

About ten days before they left the White House, Mrs. Coolidge told a story to the ladies who lived at Congress Hall Hotel. When Coolidge was in the Massachusetts State Senate, a smooth-tongued book agent sold Mrs. Coolidge a homebook of medicine for $6. She felt soon afterward that she had made a mistake, but she placed the book on the library table. Mr. Coolidge read the book before dinner and for two or three evenings thereafter. Then she put it on the book shelf and for years never looked at it. It was still on the library shelf when she was packing to leave the White House. For some reason she thought to look inside the book. She found on the flyleaf in President Coolidge's handwriting this inscription: "I don't find any cure for suckers." She said she would have died before she would have let him know she had seen it, after all those years.

Finis Garrett

Finis Garrett of Tennessee was designated by Claude Kitchin as acting floor leader after Kitchin suffered a stroke while speaking in the well of the House. Garrett later became floor leader. When the President made a personal appearance to address a Joint Session of the Congress it was the custom of newspapermen to interview the floor leaders and ask them to comment on the President's speech. Usually the President's partisans would laud the speech and the opposite side would belittle it. The incident I am now recalling occurred while Frank Mondell was Majority Floor Leader and Finis Garrett was Minority Floor Leader.

President Coolidge once delivered a 45-minute address before a joint session of the Congress. In many different ways the President stressed the need for economy. He advocated no new legislation. At the end of the President's address, Republican Floor Leader Mondell was asked to comment. He thought it was a great speech, just what the country needed.

Garrett, the Minority Floor Leader, sought to avoid saying anything by slipping out of the House and eluding newsmen. He did not think there was much he could appropriately say. Three or four newsmen caught him just as he was leaving the building, asking what he thought of the President's address. Mr. Garrett paused a moment, looking rather serious, and then said, "Longitude, latitude, and platitude."

Coolidge and Farm Legislation

In December, 1926, the House Committee reported favorably my bill to authorize the Department of Agriculture to engage in research into new uses and new markets and outlets for cotton. Cotton was having problems arising not only from increased production but also from newly developing synthetic fabrics. The bill was passed and signed by President Coolidge early in 1927; I was presented the pen with which the measure was signed.

Much good work was done by the Department under this measure. The research division helped in the blending of cotton with wool, mohair and other natural basic fabrics and with some of the synthetics; it also assisted in developing better varieties of all cotton cloth. During 1927 I introduced a general measure to authorize the establishment of regional research laboratories in each of the major producing areas of the United States. These were not established until several years later, although I introduced similar measures at the beginning of each Congress.

The McNary-Haugen farm bill was twice passed by the Congress and twice vetoed by President Coolidge. It had a provision for a tax or fee — called an equalization fee — to be paid on the first sale of farm commodities. The proceeds of the fee were to be paid to exporters in order to encourage exportation of farm commodities. The bill, however, had no provision to discourage over-production. It was a very controversial measure but it made people realize the need to bring agriculture back to a basis of equality with the rest of the economy.

Congressman John C. Ketcham of Michigan, L. J. Taber of the National Grange and I worked several days drafting a simpler and more direct measure. Our substitute bill provided that, when any farmer, cooperative organization of farmers, or others, shipped any basic farm commodity abroad, the shipper should be issued a negotiable certificate in an amount equal to the average tariff on manufactured commodities of equal value, and that these certificates should be tenderable in payment of any tariff duties on any imported article. The exporting farm organizations or farmer could sell the certificate to an importer. This, of course, would stimulate the exportation of farm commodities and, by disposing of the surplus, raise the farmers' domestic price. The farmer would be given the benefit of any tariff law that might be in effect. The first veto had created such a storm that the President was anxious to avoid another.

President Coolidge asked Ketcham, Mr. Taber, and me to see him about our substitute for the pending bill. We expected to be called upon to explain it to him, but to our surprise he knew practically all the provisions. Despite his reputation for taciturnity, he did about three-fourths of the talking during the 30- or 40-minute interview. He told us that he recognized the serious farm problem; he felt it would be improper for him to threaten veto; Attorney-General Mitchell had advised him the McNary-Haugen bill was unconstitutional; but he would go as far as he could in support of our bill. He said he would be willing for us to repeat to the Congress what he had said, and he said he would be glad to have us do so. We offered our substitute, but it was narrowly defeated; the second McNary-Haugen bill passed and was again given a blazing veto.

Chapter XIII

1928 AND THE DEPRESSION

IN THE 1928 CAMPAIGN the Republicans nominated Herbert C. Hoover of California and the Democrats nominated Alfred E. Smith of New York. It was the bitterest campaign I have ever witnessed. It gave me the only serious opposition I had in my twenty-four years of service in the Congress.

Mr. Smith was a Catholic, and there was an intense feeling at that time against electing a Catholic as President. Fortunately, that prejudice has now almost entirely disappeared, but the feeling was strong in 1928. To complicate matters, Mr. Smith was in favor of greatly liberalizing the immigration laws; the South and West largely favored restricted immigration. Furthermore, Mr. Smith favored repeal of the Eighteenth Amendment; Mr. Hoover said the Amendment was an experiment noble in purpose and far-reaching in effect, and that he wished it to succeed. Persons strongly moved by prejudice against Catholicism would give other reasons for opposing Smith.

Many Democratic Congressmen were in deep trouble, and a number of good men were defeated. An able district attorney named J. Ross Bell ran against me in the primary, held in July 1928. He campaigned all over the district's fifty-three counties prior to the Democratic National Convention in June, proclaiming his opposition to the nomination of Al Smith; I made no statement on that subject before the Convention. When Congress adjourned just before the Convention, I announced that as a Democrat I would support the entire Democratic ticket from constable to President; I supported Smith consistently throughout the campaign. My opponent said nothing more about Mr. Smith, but he was generally known as a "Hoovercrat."

In the six weeks prior to the primary election, I spoke three or four times per day. One curious sidelight of my campaign was the fact that my opponent had an identical twin brother, Tom Bell. They looked almost exactly alike. They campaigned separately over the district. Occasionally one of my friends would tell me he had seen my opponent at Perryton at the same time another had seen him hundreds of miles away. In fairness, I think they did not openly misrepresent the situation. In the enthusiasm of political gatherings, people just gained the impression that the twin was the candidate in person. They were both excellent speakers, and were good men.

Opposition to Mr. Smith was noisy, well-financed, and sometimes almost vicious. Somehow I was fortunate; I defeated Bell in the primary by a larger margin than I had expected, about 52,000 to 26,000. The campaign for Mr. Hoover continued until the general election, at which time he carried Texas by some 75,000 and my district by more than 10,000. Fortunately, the Democrats had learned to split their tickets, and I was reelected by a larger majority than I had won in the primary. Hoover won the Presidency by a large majority.

One of the most colorful of all the Congressmen was Claude Hudspeth of El Paso; in 1928 he was forced to make the same kind of fight I had to make. At one of his speaking engagements, a constituent expressed opposition to Smith because he feared the Pope wanted to control the country. Mr. Hudspeth retorted, "No, if the Pope had wanted this country, he would have bought it when Harry Daugherty had it for sale." This was just four years after the Teapot Dome scandals; Harry Daugherty had been Harding's Attorney General, and many charged him with being implicated.

For several months after Hoover took office, there apparently was great prosperity. The stock market enjoyed "the great Hoover Bull Market." On a black day in late November 1929, the great crash came. Stock prices in some cases dropped to one-half and some of them to less than one-third the previous day's market price. Stocks rallied for a few days, and then the bottom fell out again, and the great depression deepened. Many thought this was like other financial panics and could last only a few months, but such was not the case.

In 1930, the Committee on Agriculture was considering a bill providing for livestock loans, which I did not think was adequate.

I drafted another bill which the committee sent to the Secretary of Agriculture, Arthur M. Hyde, for the Department's reaction; it provided for regional agricultural organizations over the country which could make loans suitable to the needs of livestock producers. Mr. Hyde liked my proposed measure and, in spite of the fact that I was then a member of the minority party, he recommended its passage. It was passed by the House and Senate and approved by the President on March 3, 1931. The Act proved a boon to livestock people; with loans at reasonable rates, the growers could continue operations. This system operated successfully for a number of years, and was finally absorbed in the Farm Credit Administration Act which I helped to draft and sponsored through the Congress some years later. President Hoover presented me the pen with which he had signed the measure. After the election of November 1930, the Republicans and Democrats were equally divided in the House. It was not certain which party would organize the Congress to convene March 4, 1931. The Twentieth, or "Lame Duck" Amendment had not been ratified. The Democrats organized the House and chose John Nance Garner of Texas as Speaker; I became Chairman of the Committee on Agriculture.

While President Hoover did not make many legislative proposals, he did request the establishment of the Reconstruction Finance Corporation, stipulating that loans made through it be limited to banks, railroads, and insurance and mortgage companies. There was lively discussion of the bill in the House. I offered an amendment making any concern or individual eligible for RFC loans. No money was available anywhere in the nation; the difficulty was not limited to banks, railroads, and mortgage companies; the whole economy was locked and gradually sinking.

After the spirited fight, my amendment was defeated, and the bill was passed; and, just as we had predicted, the banks and mortgage and insurance companies in many instances used the RFC money to relieve the pressure on themselves and then largely froze these assets for fear of again jeopardizing their own condition. Relief did not spread to other segments of the economy. It is one thing for the government to give an open chance to the economy;

but it is another thing entirely for the government in a great emergency to pour risk money into limited channels without seeing that the benefits are passed on.

The depression grew worse. Even the banks and mortgage companies began to suffer from the stagnant conditions. During the winter of 1932 the suffering became indescribable. Banks collapsed daily by the score. Farms were being foreclosed by the thousands. There was little work and practically no ready money. Millions of people were hungry, helpless, hopeless, and despairing. This distress was especially present in our great farm states. In some places violence came close to the surface and sometimes erupted.

I was very happy in 1931 when my friend from boyhood days, the Honorable Robert Ewing Thomason of El Paso, was elected to the Congress. His father and my father were good friends, and when as a young man Ewing was a candidate for prosecuting attorney my father enthusiastically supported him. Our homes were only six miles apart, and our careers paralleled in many respects. We were both graduated from Southwestern University and from the Law School of the University of Texas; we served together in the Congress, and we both later became United States judges. Ewing Thomason served in the Texas Legislature, where he was elected Speaker; he later served as Mayor of El Paso before coming to Congress.

Chapter XIV

THE 1932 CAMPAIGN

A LARGE NUMBER of candidates were vying for the Democratic nomination in 1932: Franklin D. Roosevelt, Governor of New York; Al Smith; Carter Glass, backed by the Virginia delegation; Albert C. Ritchie of Maryland; John Nance Garner; and Newton D. Baker, who was considered quite able and who had strong backing.

In early spring before Garner's name had become prominent, Sam Rayburn and I discussed his chances. Garner had not said he wanted it, but I knew he did. He and I lived at the same hotel, and we used to play bridge together. After our chat, Rayburn went to see Garner. Later Rayburn delivered a speech to the Texas State convention which helped to secure the Texas delegation's endorsement of Garner.

The California delegation was also for John Garner, at the behest of William G. McAdoo. McAdoo was interested primarily in scotching Al Smith's renomination. He still held a grudge against Al Smith, who had kept him from being nominated in 1924. He felt that he could have won the Presidency, because the stage was all set for a Democratic victory that year, and the prolonged and bitter fight in the Democratic convention frittered the opportunity away.

I think McAdoo had more to do with Garner's getting the California delegation than any other person or group. He was very partial to John Garner. Garner could gauge what the House would do better than anybody else I ever served with. President Wilson, the father-in-law of William G. McAdoo, relied a great deal on Garner. Throughout the Wilson administration, Garner had been one of Wilson's standbys. The President frequently asked him to help pass legislation in which he was interested. It was thus natural that McAdoo should feel very close to Garner.

I think there is no doubt that McAdoo also had William G. McAdoo in the back of his mind. He was a man of tremendous capacity and overweening ambition, and he still felt that he had a chance.

He felt that if affairs shaped themselves properly, it would be natural for him to be nominated. At the same time, he was fond of John Garner, and, if he weren't going to be nominated himself, I think he would rather have had Garner than anybody else in the country.

There were several people who mentioned Roosevelt to me. Some member of the New York delegation, perhaps John F. Carew, was the first. There was a lot of talk about Roosevelt at the time. He was elected Governor of New York in 1928, the same year Al Smith lost New York and the Presidency. I told all of them from the beginning that, while I was for Garner if he could be nominated, I would like to see Franklin D. Roosevelt nominated. I know Mr. Rayburn felt the same way. Many of the members of the House felt that Roosevelt was the real hope of the party and that since he evidently had the Empire State on his side, it would be easier to win with him than with any other person. Then, too, he had the reputation of being somewhat liberal, and everybody felt that something pretty drastic had to be done to get the country out of the desperate condition to which it had sunk.

There was quite a fight at the convention. If Roosevelt hadn't been nominated just when he was, he might not have made it. I did not attend the Convention, but I was keeping in touch. I talked to one or two in Chicago on the night of the trade between Garner and the Roosevelt forces, but not to the ones who were doing the job. It wasn't any secret in Washington that James A. Farley and his group were trying to get Garner and McAdoo to cast their support to Roosevelt and then nominate Garner for Vice President.

Garner had never said he would accept the Vice Presidency; many thought he would rather be Speaker of the House than to be Vice President. They had a hard time reaching him in Washington, because he always retired early and left word he was not to be disturbed. I think it was Rayburn who finally talked to Garner. They could talk pretty frankly to each other. Garner sputtered around a little I think, but finally he said that while he did not want to make any trade, if they wanted to nominate him for Vice President, he would accept it. McAdoo first announced the switch of

California and Texas votes to Roosevelt.

I talked to Garner several times about the nomination. He felt that no man in public life has the right to decline a call to duty. He preached that throughout his public life. He jumped me once in the late twenties because I would not get off the Agricultural Committee to become chairman of the new Veterans Committee. He thought I should come at the leadership's call, but I chose to stay on Agriculture. I think he did not expect to be nominated for the Presidency, and he felt honored that he was to be nominated for the Vice Presidency. He was very partial to me. I was very fond of him and had great admiration for him.

Al Smith took Roosevelt's nomination harder than anyone else. He had felt he was entitled to renomination, and that this was the year the Democrats were going to win — and it was. I think Hoover's unpopularity was so great that almost any Democrat could have won.

I really didn't get well acquainted with Governor Roosevelt until the campaign began. Tom Connally and I went up with Silliman Evans to see him at Albany early in the campaign. We arrived at the Mansion about 9:30 in the morning. That was the first time I ever met Mrs. Roosevelt. A press conference was to be held at 10 o'clock. We offered to excuse ourselves, but the Governor insisted we stay. This was the first press conference I ever heard Roosevelt conduct; I saw right away that he was a wizard at it. There must have been 20 or 30 newspapermen in attendance. Among other things, they were trying to get him to state his position on the bonus, which was a real issue then. He good-naturedly stalled them off, promising to make an announcement on Thursday of the following week.

After the news conference the Governor invited us to have lunch with him. Tom Connally sat at Roosevelt's right and I sat at Mrs. Roosevelt's right. The Roosevelt daughter and one of the boys, young Franklin I think, were there. We had quite a conversation during lunch. We talked about politics mainly and various political characters. Roosevelt paid quite a compliment to Burton K. Wheeler, who was very close to the Governor at that time; they later had a little disagreement. That was the first time I had been to Albany, and I got rather well acquainted with Roosevelt on that visit.

As Chairman of the Agriculture Committee, the Democratic National Committee sent me not only into many of the Western States but also into a number of Northern and Eastern States. It was easy that year to make an effective Democratic speech on agriculture. We had 5-cent cotton, 20-cent corn, and 30-cent wheat; the price of practically every farm product was below the cost of production. Hoover had promised a chicken in every pot and two cars in every garage, but after four years he sat baffled, looking around the corner for prosperity, while surplus food piled up and farm mortgages were being foreclosed.

In contrast, the Democrats had nominated a vigorous candidate with a golden voice, a sparkling personality, and a record of accomplishment, who was assuring people that he would at least take action to remedy the desperate situation. At first I thought Roosevelt was a little breezy. He gave that impression when you first met him. He was very friendly; when he was amused, as he frequently was, he would throw back his head and laugh. It did not take him but about two minutes to begin calling you by your given name. But as soon as you began to talk to him about public affairs, you saw that there was great substance to him and that he had a marvelous knowledge of public affairs as well as a deep and serious interest in them. He had a wonderful personality which soon dispelled any unfavorable first impression. He fascinated me and I think nearly everybody else who had a chance to be with him much.

Roosevelt campaigned thoroughly. He flew to the Convention and accepted the nomination, having written his acceptance speech while on the plane. He had a stormy trip to Chicago, but arrived safely and was given a tremendous ovation after his speech. M. L. Wilson and one or two others talked to him during the campaign and sold him on the idea of the processing fee. He said he was for a farm measure and that he was going to get the farm groups together and enlist their help in preparing appropriate legislation. He outlined different things that it must include. It had to be a measure that would assure the farmers a better price. It had to be self-supporting; that is, it had to carry its own financing. He had about six or seven different requirements that the farm plan must have. Of course, he campaigned also on government economy and many other things.

Roosevelt and Garner were overwhelmingly elected. Soon after his election he went to Warm Springs for a rest. In the meantime, conditions were growing steadily worse. Farm foreclosures were on the increase, and the prices of farm products were still far below the cost of production. I returned to Washington in December to attend the last short session of Congress under the Hoover administration.

One of the problems President Roosevelt inherited from the previous administration was the drive to pay in cash the deferred service bonus. In 1924, the Congress passed a deferred bonus bill which provided for payments in twenty years to each veteran for each month he had served. A veterans' movement was organized and marched on Washington to demand immediate cash payment. They came in great numbers from all over the nation. They camped in vacant buildings around the Capitol and stayed. President Hoover ordered General McArthur and the Army to drive the bonus marchers out of Washington and across the river, and there they camped again.

Texas Congressman Wright Patman introduced a bill providing immediate cash payment of the bonus. The Congress passed the bill, but President Hoover vetoed it. The Congress tried but could not override the veto. President Roosevelt also vetoed the bill when it was re-enacted in 1933, and again the veto held. The bill was passed by the next Congress and was again vetoed; this time the President's veto was overridden, and the bonus was paid in cash during the mid-1930s.

Chapter XV

THE PRESIDENT-ELECT

THE NEWLY ELECTED President telephoned me in late November 1932 from Warm Springs, to tell me he was sending William I. Myers of Cornell University, Henry Morgenthau, Henry Wallace, and another man to see me; he wanted us to draft a farm bill along the lines outlined in his campaign speeches, and pass it if possible at the Lame Duck session. This was the congressional session held after the election and before the March 4 presidential inauguration. This was to be the last Lame Duck session; the new constitutional amendment would preclude others. I told Mr. Roosevelt I would do my best, but that passage might be difficult, because Mr. Hoover was still President and the equally divided Congress was intensely partisan. The President-elect had handed me the most difficult assignment I would probably ever face.

The group came the next day. We spent two days on the farm bill, working on a draft I had previously prepared. Henry Morgenthau had to leave early; he told me privately that I was better informed than the others, that he would tell Mr. Roosevelt so, and that I should have the final say as to the terms of the bill. I introduced our bill on the first day of the session; the Agriculture Committee held hearings and reported the bill favorably. The House took up the bill early in January 1933.

In my initial speech in support of the measure, I phrased the nation's dilemma:

> We as Americans are unwilling victims of the strangest famine ever recorded in the annals of civilization. Barns bursting with plenty and yet millions of hungry people are walking the streets of our cities. The farmer cannot sell at a living price, and in many instances the man in the city cannot purchase at any price.

Some features of the bill were entirely new, and there was much opposition to it, especially on the processing tax. The votes on amendments were very close, and the battle raged on. Hundreds of telegrams in opposition to the entire bill were pouring in. Finally the opposition secured a voice-vote adoption of a damaging amendment. John Garner suggested we wait until the next session when we would have a good majority, but I was reluctant to admit we were licked.

The Chairman of the Appropriations Committee, a Democrat, offered a preferential amendment to strike out the enacting clause, which would have killed the bill. I moved that the Committee of the Whole House rise and report progress, which amounted to an adjournment until the next day; my motion carried.

Several days before I had prepared a mimeographed explanation of the bill, which I had mailed to persons who had sent me telegrams. One I received that morning was most interesting; it gave me a great idea for the coming session that morning. When the House convened and the Chairman of the Appropriations Committee asked unanimous consent to withdraw his motion to strike out the enacting clause, I objected and asked for a showdown. And then I told the House about the telegram I had received which read, "I did not authorize my name to be put on the telegram in question. That telegram was sent by Armour & Co. I am for the allotment plan. (signed) A. H. Ahrens." I offered to show the telegram to anyone interested. I then argued that, while I did not oppose big business, I felt they had no right to run the Congress.

When I had finished my speech, the motion to strike was defeated, 100 yeas to 161 nays. After that, the bill passed the House, 253 ayes to 151 nays on January 18, 1932. Congressman Hatton Sumners said to me that it was the most dramatic scene he had ever witnessed in the House, and that my short speech was the most effective he had ever heard. John Garner was much pleased. He later told the President-elect that I was one of the ablest legislators in the Congress and was a floor manager of great skill.

Representatives of the packers came to me later and explained that they had made an error and used the name of the wrong man. I offered to make their explanation on the floor, but I added that more talk would necessarily confirm their propaganda campaign against the bill and their haste in securing signatures. They asked me not to comment further on the situation; they had merely wanted me to know the facts.

In February 1933, Mr. Roosevelt's train, en route from New York to Warm Springs, stopped in Washington, and I met with him on the back platform of his car. He thought I had done a grand job in securing the passage of the farm bill through the House; he smiled and said, "You must be a magician." He hoped I could get the bill through the Senate before March 4 but I told him there was little hope of that. I felt we would be able to get action in the new Congress which would soon convene. The photographers took pictures of us standing on the back platform of his special car. One of these photographs is a prized possession of mine, and is reproduced in the picture section.

The depression grew worse. By early 1933 banks began to go broke by the hundreds; farm mortgages were being foreclosed by the thousands. By inauguration day a gloom amounting almost to despair had settled over the entire country. Shortly before the inauguration, Henry Morgenthau told me Governor Roosevelt wanted me to work with William I. Myers of Cornell University to write an executive order pulling out of the various departments of government all of the agencies that had been lending money to farmers, placing all of them in a single independent agency.

I had never written an executive order. We got the job done, but I must admit that most of the credit is due to Dr. Myers. He was a technician and an administrator of great skill, and we worked together on many problems thereafter as long as Cornell University permitted him to remain on leave. We named the new agency the Farm Credit Administration. The President signed the Executive Order a few days later.

Advance assignments like those I performed were given to chairmen of some of the other major committees. It was evident the new President was to be a man of action. This was in bright contrast to the bafflled inaction of his predecessor.

Horace K. Jones
father of Marvin.

Docia Gaston
Hawkins Jones
mother of Marvin.

President Woodrow Wilson about 1918.

Champ Clark, former Speaker and erstwhile presidential aspirant, circa 1918.

"Uncle Joe" Cannon, former Speaker, about 1918.

James R. Mann, Republican Leader in the 1920s, friend and mentor of young Jones.

Congressman Marvin Jones, Chairman of the House Committee on Agriculture, with Senator Ellison (Cotton Ed) Smith, Chairman of the Senate Committee on Agriculture, and Secretary of Agriculture Henry A. Wallace, in the mid-1930s.

John Nance Garner, Speaker of the House and later Vice-President.

Four Presidents at the funeral of S

KENNEDY   JOHNSON

Others in attendance included Judg

n Rayburn in 1961 in Bonham, Texas

EISENHOWER　　　　　TRUMAN

Jones, second from left on third row.

James F. Byrnes, Director of Economic Stabilization, and Marvin Jones, War Food Administrator, during World War II.

Judge Marvin Jones, President Harry S. Truman, and Speaker Sam Rayburn, about 1950.

Mrs. Jeff M. Neely (Metze) of Amarillo and her brother Judge Marvin Jones of the U. S. Court of Claims at the unveiling of his portrait in Washington, October 23, 1968.

Chapter XVI

THE NEW PRESIDENT

An immense crowd came to the inauguration on March 4, 1933. It was a colorful occasion. President Roosevelt's inspiring address seemed to breathe new life and hope not only into the assembled multitude but into all the millions who were listening in. He capped it with the famous phrase, "The only thing we have to fear is fear itself."

The people of the country became confident again. The President, on the second or the third evening after taking office, gave the first of his fireside chats over radio. His golden voice and his personality captivated people everywhere. I heard many say he seemed to be talking directly to them.

One of his first acts as President was to close the banks. It was a master stroke, designed to stop bank failures. The banks would be reopened as rapidly as they could be examined and found to be sound. Some people were caught without money, but they did not seem to mind.

I was given the task of sponsoring the first major bill in the new Congress. Prior to the inauguration, the President had asked the heads of the three principal farm organizations to get together and agree on a bill. They had been sponsoring different measures. He had facetiously told them he was going to lock them up together until they agreed. Their bill followed along the lines of the bill which I had piloted through the House in the Lame Duck session, which levied a fee on the processing of basic farm commodities to provide subsidies to the farmers.

I had taught constitutional law at the University of Texas; I knew that a tax could not be levied on one group and the proceeds paid directly to another. I insisted that the proceeds of the tax be paid directly into the United States Treasury, and that an estimated similar amount be appropriated out of the general funds of the Treasury. We provided also for compensation to the farmers for engaging in soil conservation and soil building practices.

Another provision I insisted upon was for county and community committees of farmers with broad administrative authority in the program. I had quite a discussion of this point with one of the bright young men who came to Washington with the new President. He insisted it would be simpler and more economical to lay out the whole program and make all the decisions in Washington. I told him that it was a beautiful theory, but that it would simply not work in practice.

I insisted that the county committees be selected in each county by a vote of the farmers themselves. They would know their neighbors and local conditions. In the event of unfair decisions, appeals could be arranged, but I felt that decisions should only be reversed when shown to be clearly unfair. I am told that some time after World War II, Washington officials began to take away some of the authority of the local committees. I hope the committees have not been stripped of responsibility. It is impossible for a Washington administration to fashion a program to fit the entire nation. It saddens me to see the tendency to center all power and authority in Washington.

Since we had conducted full hearings on a similar bill in the Lame Duck session only a few weeks before, we now held only brief hearings and soon reported the measure to the House. We had a good working majority, and the Committee had little trouble in securing passage by the House in record time. However, it took several weeks to secure final passage in the Senate.

Refinancing Farm Mortgages

I introduced the bill for refinancing farm mortgages. The Agriculture Committee conducted a few days' hearing, and there was astonishing interest in the measure. A crowd of more than 500 overflowed the committee room and filled the hallway halfway down its length. Many of them wanted to testify. I held an interview in my office for a few minutes before the hearing began. Representatives from various farm groups and many others crowded in, filling the office. I could talk only with group spokesmen; if I had undertaken to hear every individual, many farmers would have lost their farms before the legislation could be passed.

Many people were crowded around where I was standing. Many stragglers and strangers had pushed their way into my office. I had to press through the crowd to make my way into the committee room. It was an orderly hearing, but just before noon I reached for my watch to compare its time with the clock on the wall, and the watch was gone. It was a solid gold watch, with the head mold of ex-Governor Ross of Texas in gold riveted on the back with gold rivets. I had won it in an oratorical contest at the University of Texas. Naturally, I was very proud of it. Although I advertised extensively, offering liberal rewards, it was never found. It could not be replaced, because the Boston firm that had made the mold had gone out of business, and the mold could not be found.

We soon closed the hearings. The committee went over the bill in executive session and then reported it. It was passed in the House and sent to the Senate before they had acted on the Agricultural Adjustment Act, which had been sent to the Senate some time earlier.

The Farm Credit Reference Battle

In early April 1933 the President requested the House to pass a measure collecting under one agency all kinds of agricultural credit. Since the measure he desired included the broadening of the operations of the Federal Land Banks, it would normally have been referred to the Banking and Currency Committee which had handled the previous legislation establishing the original Federal and Intermediate Credit Banks. The proposed measure, however, included all forms of agricultural credit.

I told the Speaker I wanted to offer a privileged motion to refer the entire message to the Agriculture Committee instead of to the Banking and Currency Committee. He tried to discourage me, but I persisted. I called for action on the motion on April 4, 1933. It was strongly opposed by the Chairman and Members of the Banking and Currency Committee and some of the other House leaders. Henry Steagall, Chairman of the Banking and Currency Committee, asked that I consent to wait until the next day so he could look up the precedents. After securing assurance from the Speaker that he would not refer the bill to any committee before final action on the motion, I readily agreed.

The next day we had a tremendous battle. The other side argued that the precedents of the House should not be upset; that the Banking and Currency Committee had handled the Land Bank and other farm credit legislation; that this was primarily a banking and currency question; and that its committee was experienced in such matters. I pleaded that loans to farmers and livestock producers were entirely different from business loans; that there should be a system of loans entirely separate from the commercial credit structure geared primarily to the needs of business; that the Banking and Currency Committee had done fine work in connection with the business world, but it had been very busy with those matters and had neglected the ruinously high interest rates which had been wrecking the operations of the farm and ranch; that we needed a new deal in the financial world; and that such a change was long overdue. Many members joined in urging that the message be referred to the Agriculture Committee.

Mr. Steagall made a speech in opposition, urging that this would change the precedents of the House; that the Banking and Currency Committee had been handling the legislation that established the land banks and their credit needs; that this would almost be like legislating by resolution. Members who spoke for the resolution of reference alternated with those who spoke against it. Mr. Goldsborough's attack on the measure was almost vicious, and some of those who were for it argued in strong terms. These speeches are all included in the *Congressional Record*. Mr. Luce of Massachusetts, a member of the Banking and Currency Committee, made a strong analysis of the proposed bill. Those favoring the motion said the interest rates were too high and that the bill should be handled by the Committee that was directly interested in the legislation. Strong arguments were made on both sides. I made the concluding argument in favor of the motion.

To the surprise of many, the motion was carried by a vote of 172 to 83. Since that action, the Committee on Agriculture has handled agricultural credit matters.

The Farm Credit Administration Bill

Dr. William I. Myers and I drafted a bill to implement the independent and separate Farm Credit Administration, which had been decreed by executive order, and was to be given authority to issue and sell obligations and impose essential regulations so it could handle the different types of farm credit. When the Committee finished the draft, we sent the President a copy about noon and he asked to see us the next day. He was exceedingly busy seeing delegation after delegation every day. We went to see him at 11 o'clock. In a very few minutes after we arrived, a group of businessmen came out of his office and we went in.

We had expected the President to ask what was in the bill, but he reached over, took the copy of the bill out of his desk, and began asking searching questions. He would say, "Why did you put in section 8?" Or, "What is the exact connection with section 7? Is the interest rate as low as we can get it, and still stay on a sound basis?" He knew all about the provisions of the bill. How he found time even to read the bill was a mystery, but he knew exactly what he wanted to ask. At that time when everyone wanted action, he was able to keep up. He was an amazing person. After discussion he expressed approval of our bill.

The bill had four parts. It established twelve regional cooperative banks to finance the operations of cooperative organizations of farmers and twelve regional production credit corporations for financing livestock producers. It provided for expanding and better financing of the twelve regional Federal Land Banks, and for twelve Intermediate Credit Discount Banks, which were placed in charge of the marketing of the obligations and long-range financing of the regional operations of the banks and Production Credit Corporations. It authorized an appropriation of $200,000,000 to aid in getting the agency in full operation as quickly as possible. These funds were to be repaid to the Government. It also included a continuance of the Regional Agriculture Credit Corporation and the Crop Loan Act, both of which I had sponsored earlier and which had been in effect some time.

The entire operation has been a striking success from the start. Theretofore, farmers had paid annual interest rates as high as 22 percent. The measures we enacted reduced interest rates an average of nearly 40 percent. And even more surprising, the advance funds were repaid to the United States with interest. For all practical purposes, the operations of the various organizations are financed substantially through sales in the open commercial market without cost or risk to the Government. The Production Credit Corporations were the first to pay back all the advance funds several years ago, but all segments of the organization are operating on a solid financial basis.

Much credit is due Dr. Myers, a truly great administrator who stayed in charge until the lending agency was well established in a very successful operation. He was then called back to Cornell University. All those interested in this work regretted that it became necessary for him to leave.

When the bill, which carried my name, was signed on June 14, 1933, it was the boyhood dream finally realized. The President gave me the pen with which the bill was signed. Only one pen was used in that instance, and it is on display in the Panhandle Plains Historical Building at Canyon, Texas.

A Three-Titled Bill

At one point, the three major bills which I had sponsored through the House were still on the Senate calendar before final passage. The President, on advice of financial experts, had reduced the gold content of the dollar as one of the several steps in relieving the tight money situation.

When the original Agriculture bill, which I had handled in the passage through the House, and the Farm Credit bill, of which I was joint author, and which had now been merged with the emergency farm refinancing measure, reached the Senate, that body decided to combine these measures; and then they added the Thomas bill to reduce the gold content of the dollar, and thus expand the currency, all in one bill with three separate titles. They made the AAA, the original farm act which we had sent over, into Title I, then attached the farm refinancing bill as Title II and the marketing of government obligations and gold content measure as Title III. The three-titled measure was passed by the Senate early in June 1933.

The House Committee on Agriculture decided that, since the first two titles now contained the two bills exactly as they had passed the House and the third title seemed desirable and was approved by the Administration, we would simply agree to the Senate amendment adding Title III.

I offered a motion to agree to the Senate amendment and pass the triple measure. This made a conference unnecessary. We were all anxious for early passage of the measures as a part of the effort to get the economy moving following the broken years from which it was just emerging. My motion was adopted by the House June 10, 1933, and the bill was approved by the President June 14, 1933.

Chapter XVII

THE FIRST HUNDRED DAYS

  Much has been written about the "First Hundred Days" of the Roosevelt administration. I had the privilege of handling more major bills in their passage through the House during those one hundred days than any other member of the Congress. These included the Agricultural Adjustment and Soil Conservation Act, the Act for Refinancing of Farm Mortgages, the Farm Credit Administration Act, and the measure reducing the gold content of the dollar. I was greatly assisted by the members of the loyal and hard-working Agriculture Committee, in which there was practically no partisanship. The condition of the country was entirely too serious and the emergency too great for petty bickering.

Of course, other bills were passed during the one hundred days, such as the acts establishing the National Recovery Administration (NRA), the Works Progress Administration (WPA), the Resettlement Administration and the Public Works Administration (PWA), which were handled by other committees.

The President's Official Conferences

About three days after his inauguration, President Roosevelt asked the Speaker, the Vice President and the chairmen of the major committees to come to the White House for a conference at 8 o'clock in the evening. The President said he wanted to talk with us about his plans and hopes for passing essential legislation. He then outlined what he hoped might help in restoring the country, urging us to speak out on anything in which we were interested.

He then discussed the various measures he wanted to have enacted. He seemed to have the whole program of recovery in his mind. Several of us asked questions. There was a general discussion, and the conference lasted until 11 o'clock. It was a most interesting session. It gave us all an across-the-board picture of what was to be recommended and a better understanding of all phases of the recovery program. For the first year he had similar meetings every month. We looked forward to these conferences. They enabled us to keep abreast of how the legislation each Committee was handling fitted into the whole pattern.

Repeal of Prohibition

Soon after the inauguration, the President requested that the Congress submit an amendment to the Constitution providing for the repeal of the 18th Amendment. He sent a strong message urging early action. A joint resolution was passed by the Congress on February 20, 1933. It was shortly thereafter ratified by three-fourths of the States and became effective on December 5, 1933.

Many years later at a meeting of the National Judicial Conference in the Supreme Court building in Washington, I had lunch with a United States circuit judge from Minnesota who was soon to retire. He asked me if I knew Andrew J. Volstead, the Minnesotan who sponsored the 1919 legislation to enforce the Prohibition Amendment. I said yes, that I had served with him in Congress several years. The judge then told me of six dry Texans who crossed his state's border into Canada to quench their thirst. On the way back they stopped for lunch and while they were eating some mischievous boys wrote in white letters on the back of the car:

> There was a band of Texans
> And they were very dry.
> They went into Canada
> To get a little rye.
> When the rye was opened
> They all began to sing
> Who the hell is Volstead?
> God save the King!

Financing Federal Land Banks

For years the Federal Reserve Board had been authorizing the issuance of Federal Reserve notes by its member banks. As assurance of security and liquidity, the applicant bank was required to furnish a specified amount of selected commercial notes held by it plus a specified amount of Government bonds. The bank complying was required to pay a small administrative charge and a small tax.

I told President Roosevelt that, since at that time 30 percent of the population was engaged directly or indirectly in farming, I thought 30 percent of the $2,800,000 cash made available by reducing the gold content of the dollar should be earmarked for use by the Federal Farm Land Banks. These banks could put up a designated amount of the mortgage notes plus the required gold as security. The President thought this was a very interesting idea and suggested that I get someone to help me draw it up in bill form. I secured a real expert, who drafted a bill incorporating the ideas I had outlined and took the proposed bill back to the President. He then told me he had already committed all the gold savings to other pressing purposes and suggested that perhaps we could work out something else.

I still wanted in some way to make a portion of the advantages which commercial banks enjoy available to the Land Banks. I realized that all the needs of the Land Banks could not be financed in this way, but neither are all the needs of commercial banks. If even a small portion of land paper could be financed by this method on a short-term basis, it would reduce the over-all farm interest rates. It would be especially helpful at times when the Federal Land Banks find it necessary to sell bonds during periods of high interest rates.

To finish up this subject in one place, I may add that one of the last measures I sponsored in the House many years later dealt with an effort to extend the limited rediscount privilege to the Federal Land Banks. A member of the Federal Reserve Board, an attorney for that organization, and other students of finance told me that, properly safeguarded, the plan would work.

The Home Owners Loan Corporation

In view of the vast number of homes lost in towns and cities by reason of mortgage foreclosures, the Congress passed a measure establishing the Home Owners Loan Corporation, which provided for a board with authority to establish banks throughout the nation to refinance the mortgages on homes in danger of foreclosure. The board decided to establish four banks in Texas. It was generally assumed they would be located in the four leading cities of the state. Former Congressman W. F. Stevenson was made Chairman of the National Board; I had served with him and knew him to be an able man and a good administrator.

I went before him to propose that one of the banks be located in Amarillo. It was the central point of a large area of approximately 100 counties; it was more than three hundred miles from the nearest of the four principal cities of the state and nearly eight hundred miles from the most distant. I emphasized that the Panhandle-Plains area ranged from 3,000 to more than 4,000 feet above sea level, and that more compactly built housing facilities were essential because of the colder weather.

Amarillo was selected as one of the four locations. It was manned by local people who understood the needs of the area, with a representative in each county to send in applications and provide appraisals. Two outstanding young attorneys, John Fullingim and Rip C. Underwood, were appointed as counsel. The bank was a lifesaver to that section. Thousands of homes were refinanced and saved in that area during the first year of its operation.

The Conchas Dam

For many years A. S. (Syd) Stinnett of Amarillo had been interested in impounding the water of the Canadian River, which ran through New Mexico, Texas, and Oklahoma, as a flood-control and conservation measure. We visited many sites during those years. During the first year of the new Administration, the reduction of the gold content of the dollar had made two billion eight hundred million dollars available for expenditure by the Federal Government. Various works projects were established throughout the country to get this money into general circulation. We urged the inclusion of the proposed Conchas Dam in this program.

Senators Dennis Chavez and Carl Hatch of New Mexico, Carl Hinton, Secretary of the Amarillo Chamber of Commerce, and I went to see the President to get his approval of the allocation of funds. The President asked me by name if I really wanted the dam built. I replied that I certainly did; that flood control and irrigation water would help New Mexico and the western Panhandle and help assure Amarillo a reserve water supply. He assured us he would make the allocation.

I was with the President when he signed the allocation. He said, "I am giving Amarillo some water." I was told later that a few local officials had undertaken to waive Amarillo's rights to the water. It is very doubtful whether they had any authority to do so or whether their action, if taken, would be effective. However, in view of the Meredith Dam, now in operation, and other reservoirs, it may not be needed for many years. But this may not be true of some counties in the western Panhandle. It is still an open question.

Huey Long

One day I went over to the Senate looking for John Garner. I was in a hurry as I walked through the cloakroom when I met Huey Long coming the other way. He was apparently in a hurry also, but he called me by name and we shook hands. He said, "I've just been out to a meeting in Des Moines. I met a cousin of yours out there, J. T. Jones. He's a likely looking chap. I just thought you'd like to hear about him."

Long had been in Washington only a short time and I was surprised that he recognized me. He did things like that frequently; I would hear about similar incidents in connection with other people. Naturally, it was somewhat flattering to have a fellow mention such an incident. Huey Long was an amazing person; he had a quick, agile mind and a good memory. He evidently had a good many people gathering information for him. There never has been anybody quite like Huey Long.

Later on, five Louisiana members of the House of Representatives met secretly one night and agreed that they would oppose Huey Long's methods. He announced on the floor of the Senate the next day that five members of the Louisiana delegation had held a meeting the night before and agreed to oppose what he stood for, and that none of them would be in the next House. An interesting fact is that they all did retire. One of them, John N. Sandlin, ran for the Senate and was defeated. He was a fine fellow, too. I think one or two of them didn't run and the ones who did were defeated. At that time Huey Long had almost complete control of political affairs in Louisiana.

Cotton Ed Smith's Five-Year Plan

Senator Cotton Ed Smith of South Carolina became outraged when he realized that some of the young men in the Department of Agriculture had never worked on a farm. He introduced a resolution in the Senate in 1934 stipulating that no one should occupy a position in any policy-making division or above a certain grade in the Department of Agriculture who had not had at least five years of actual experience as a farmer.

Secretary of Agriculture Henry Wallace came to see me personally. He was as excited over that as I had ever seen him. He said a great many career men who really knew agriculture had never had actual experience in farming. I decided he was more excited than the circumstances demanded, so I facetiously suggested that perhaps three years of actual experience in farming would be enough. Then he blew up. When he had calmed down somewhat, I advised him that the Department would be wise, in making appointments, to recruit people whose heart interest was agriculture and not something else; and I told him I did not think the resolution would be seriously considered. That seemed to relieve him. I never discussed the resolution with Senator Smith, but some time afterward I kidded him a little about it.

CHAPTER XVIII

SOIL CONSERVATION AND THE FARMERS' SHARE OF THE TARIFF

DURING THE GREAT DROUTH of the early 1930s, America's largest wheat-producing area composed of the western half of Kansas and of Oklahoma, southeastern Colorado, a few counties in the northern Panhandle of Texas, and a part of New Mexico, became known as the Dust Bowl. During the great dust storms, the skies were like brass and the earth like iron; much of the top soil was blown away. Fences had caught so much sand and drifting weeds that they were completely covered. The soil had been blown until the sides of houses and barns had drifts reaching to the roof. Huge sand dunes from ten to fifteen feet high had been whipped into different hill-like shapes. The area was spreading.

No more dramatic accomplishment can be found in all history than the far-reaching series of programs under which the Dust Bowl and its expanding areas were reclaimed. Several emergency measures were necessary. I persuaded the Department of Agriculture and the Works Progress Administration (WPA) to send representatives to see the entire section. We secured an allotment of $5,000,000 for an emergency road-building program and funds for emergency relief and for shipping in feed for livestock.

The Rehabilitation Act

The Rehabilitation Act, enacted early in 1933, was designed to enable people who had been forced out of business and out of work to start anew. The commerce of the country was on dead center. We persuaded the rehabilitation authorities to establish a regional office in Amarillo to service the Dust Bowl area.

The dry weather spread to the entire country west of the Mississippi. Feed for livestock was as scarce as water, and the cattle deteriorated until most would not sell for enough to pay the freight to market. There was serious danger that all good cattle would be shipped to market and the poorer ones left to breed the livestock supply.

The Committee on Agriculture secured the appropriation of $200,000,000 to purchase poorer cattle for slaughter and distribution of the meat to relief agencies. Wherever practicable, regular packers processed the cattle, many of them at cost, and distributed the meat to hungry people in each locality. The better grades of cattle were saved.

During that time I attended the National Livestock Annual Meeting in Denver. I visited the stockyards while in Denver and was shocked at the poor condition of cattle shipped there. But these and other measures helped our country to remain one of the world's greatest producers of high quality meat.

Cowboys in Boston

In Denver a distinguished looking man introduced himself to me as James (Jim) Watson. I agreed to drive with him to Salt Lake City to attend the Western Sheep Growers meeting. The drouth was so bad we paid 10 cents a gallon twice on the trip for radiator water for his car; the service station operator at one stop told us he had hauled the water twenty miles.

Watson was a very interesting man. He was Regional Manager of the Agricultural Credit Corporation at Omaha. He had been raised by a Montana ranchman who employed orphan boys, treating them as if they were his own; the twelve or fourteen boys practically worshipped him. He usually took two of them with him to the Chicago market. Of course, they loved these trips. One especially successful year he took five boys along. The Chicago market was down and he took the shipment and the boys on to New York and sold the cattle there.

He then treated the boys to a visit to Boston, where they stayed at the Copley-Plaza Hotel. In their cowboy regalia, the boys attracted much attention. One of them was especially witty and always had a comeback. In the hotel lobby a dignified man walked up to the witty lad and asked in a rather patronizing tone, "Is this the first time you have ever seen Boston?" The wit responded, "The first time I ever even heard of it."

Unfortunately, I have forgotten the ranchman's name, but I thought the story worth telling.

Soil Work

A small amount of soil work had been done by the Departments of Agriculture and Interior, mostly in over-watered areas. I persuaded Dr. H. H. Bennett, Director of the Soil Erosion Service in Agriculture, to establish in 1935 a dry land soil project of 35,000 acres in Sherman County, Texas, one of the hardest hit counties in the Dust Bowl, with headquarters at Dalhart. The project was a tremendous success; by cover cropping, chiseling, contour plowing, and strip planting, the land was rebuilt within the project area, and it stood out in bright contrast to the surrounding land.

The National Soil Conservation Act

The scope of the original soil erosion service was very limited; by 1935, it was generally recognized that a much broader act was needed to cover soil erosion, soil wastage and soil rebuilding. Secretary of Agriculture Wallace and Secretary of Interior Ickes fought over which of them would be placed in charge of the proposed service. The Agriculture Department sent to Congress a proposed bill to establish a soil agency. Secretary Ickes proposed a complete reorganization of the Interior, calling it the "Department of Conservation and Public Works." Included in that bill was a water erosion soil provision to be administered by the reorganized department.

Wallace and Ickes both appeared before the Public Lands Committee in the fight over the location of the soil erosion activity. Wallace mentioned the "Teapot Dome" oil scandals under Secretary of the Interior Albert B. Fall as evidence that Interior might mismanage the proposed program. Secretary Ickes picked up the issue and almost won the battle right there. He was a clever fighter, and it looked as if his bill might be reported.

The Committee on Agriculture authorized me to appear before the Public Lands Committee in opposition to Ickes' bill. Secretary

Ickes was there when I testified. Most of my testimony was critical of the Ickes bill as having been drawn by a clever lawyer biased in favor of Interior.

Secretary Ickes followed me on the stand and, without answering my statement, once again dressed down Henry Wallace. The Committee then referred the bill to a subcommittee for further study. I thought Mr. Ickes would be out of humor with me, but after the hearing he smiled, shook hands, walked down the hall with me and invited me out to dinner. We became and remained very good friends. Later the President said to me Secretary Ickes had told him that I had killed his reorganization bill and had been very persuasive in doing so.

Wind Erosion

I was anxious to get the soil conservation measure through the Congress. I told my friend Jack Dempsey of New Mexico, a member of the Public Lands Committee, that I hoped to avoid the ill feeling sometimes engendered by a floor fight, but that Agriculture felt the bill would have to have a provision dealing with wind or dry-land erosion. To avoid a conflict between the Committees, we agreed on a draft of a bill and each of us introduced a copy of it; it was referred to the Committee on Agriculture, which held hearings on it. The bill was reported and passed by the Congress exactly as we had drafted it. The President gave Jack Dempsey and me each a pen used to sign the bill.

The measure has been a great success; it has had much to do with making our country the greatest food-producing nation on earth. I regard it as one of the most important measures Congress ever enacted.

The agency divided the country into ten regions along state lines, placing Louisiana, Arkansas, and all of Texas in one region. I tried to get the agency to put the Dust Bowl in a separate region where the worst of the wind erosion had occurred, but they did not want to divide any state. I thought it wrong to place the regional headquarters in the area where excess water rather than wind was the problem, but the officials declined to make the change.

I went to my good friend Chairman James P. Buchanan of the Appropriations Committee, a fellow Texan, and told him I wanted to hold up the entire soil agency appropriation. He told me the Soil Act was my baby and he would hold up the appropriation until I gave the word, but that he would have to call Dr. Bennett, the head of the new agency, and let him know.

Dr. Bennett came immediately to Buchanan's office, and I met with him and Buchanan. He was still adamant; finally I said there was no use to argue further, and the activity would have to wait a year and I started out of the room. Dr. Bennett then asked for 24 hours to work the matter out. The next morning Dr. Bennett called to say they had decided to establish the region I wanted, with Amarillo as headquarters. I told him I was very happy, but since the first experimental dry-land project had headquarters at Dalhart, Texas, I would prefer that town as headquarters. He checked that out and telephoned me later to say that quick transportation facilities were vital to good operation and that headquarters would have to be Amarillo. I could not very well protest further.

The results have been amazing. That area, instead of remaining a problem area, is now one of the nation's largest wheat and feed-crop-producing regions and is rapidly becoming one of our largest cattle feeding and marketing sections. Soil conservation and rebuilding is the life of the land, and the land is the source of food essential to all life.

The principle that conservation of soil and water resources is essential to the nation's survival is not new, but years of experimentation, demonstration, and patient work by enterprising farmers and the government were required to gain public acceptance of that principle. Before the present Soil Conservation Service was created, many thoughtful people became alarmed at the extensive damage suffered in the Dust Bowl. Very little was known then about wind erosion control.

Early in 1934 before passage of the National Soil Conservation Act, a group of Panhandle Texas county judges, commissioners, farmers, and ranchers met in the county courthouse at Dumas, during one of the worst dust storms. They drafted a pioneer piece of legislation which was enacted by the State Legislature on May 21, 1935, authorizing the creation of wind erosion conservation districts.

The act gave the district officials of the state authority to enter upon and treat neglected lands which constituted an erosion hazard; it set aside twenty percent of the state automobile registration fees and a part of state ad valorem taxes for the purpose. Wind erosion districts were promptly created in nine Texas Panhandle counties. Soon thereafter a committee from the new districts, made up of Wilson Cowen, Noel McDade, and Mal Stewart, county judges of Dallas, Moore and Deaf Smith counties, and J. O. Guleke and John E. Hill of Amarillo came to see me. I arranged a conference with M. L. Wilson, Under Secretary of Agriculture, Dr. Bennett, Chief of the newly created Soil Conservation Service, and others.

When the President's Great Plains Committee visited the Texas Panhandle, it expressed great interest in the Texas program. The Committee's report, "The Future of the Great Plains," published in 1936, commented concerning the Panhandle Wind Erosion Conservation Districts:

> It should be emphasized that the legislation adopted in Texas, despite the shortcomings indicated above, represents, nevertheless, the furthest advance which any State has made so far in the direction of establishing significant State programs for the control of soil erosion. The State has been a pioneer, and it need not be wondered that the initial efforts indicate room for improvement.

On May 13, 1936, after the Texas program had already been in successful operation, the Department of Agriculture completed its draft of a standard form of State Soil Conservation District laws, patterned on the Texas Act. President Franklin D. Roosevelt transmitted copies to the governors of the various states, asking their aid in the passage of the standard act in their states. Nearly all farm states passed the enabling legislation suggested, and more than 3,500 districts are now operating.

The foundation for all of these operations is the National Soil Conservation Act approved by the President on April 27, 1935. The first of the new districts was organized in 1937. The organization spread rapidly until it covers most of the land in our country.

Marketing Agreements

The original agricultural act had dealt mainly with the basic commodities and only incidentally with milk, fruits, vegetables and other perishables, all of which had price and marketing problems. Chester Davis, the AAA administrator, brought to my office a complicated measure which included provisions for both national and regional marketing agreements to be organized commodity by commodity. The growers and producers were to operate in production groups under the supervision and with the assistance of the Department of Agriculture. The producers of each perishable would by vote determine for themselves whether a majority of them wanted to enter such a marketing agreement for their particular commodity. It was a wide ranging and complicated bill.

I had no part in drafting this particular measure; Davis spent several hours explaining it to me. I introduced the measure and worked for its passage at his request. The bill's many new features brought on terrific fights in the House and Senate; the milk sheds were difficult to explain. After passage by both houses the bill was sent to conference.

The conference report was discussed first in the Agriculture Committee. One unique feature of the bill was that the applegrowers wanted a national marketing provision, except that Senator Byrd of Virginia, a large apple grower, had successfully led a fight in the Senate against the inclusion of a few states, especially Virginia, in the national agreements. When I mentioned in the Agriculture Committee that the conference had agreed to except Virginia from coverage by the apple section, Charles W. Tobey of New Hampshire hit the ceiling: after blowing off steam, he asked me pointblank, "Isn't this a purely political decision just to please Senator Byrd?" "No," I responded, "we were just afraid Senator Byrd would have 'appleplexy'."

In the burst of laughter that followed, Congressman Tobey made no further objection. The measure has been in effect many years and has proved very helpful in the marketing of perishables.

Some interesting exchanges between members of the House never appear in the Congressional Record. Here are two that, while they have no connection with pending legislation, appear worth recording as human interest events.

Dewey Short

Dewey Short of Missouri was in those days one of the most gifted speakers in the House. He was much in demand as a speaker and was often invited to address national conventions and organizations. He was one of the few men who ever got the better of John Rankin of Mississippi.

Dewey Short had made a trip abroad and visited many countries. In reporting to the House about his trip, his eloquence drew wide attention. John Rankin of Mississippi interrupted his oratory to dispute his facts and his conclusions, observing at the end of his comment, "I have done a good deal of traveling myself."

Congressman Short responded scornfully, "Travel! I have crawled farther under the barn looking for eggs than the gentleman from Mississippi has been away from home."

The colloquy ended in a roar of laughter.

John E. Rankin

John Rankin of Mississippi was one of the most active Members of the House for many years. He was something of a firebrand; he was rough in debate and was very good at repartee.

In one of his campaigns for reelection, he had strong opposition. Mrs. Roosevelt had very little use for Mr. Rankin and I think the feeling was reciprocated. At any rate, she gave out a statement during the campaign saying that the people of Mississippi would be wise if they kept John Rankin at home.

Of course, if he needed anything to assure his renomination or reelection, this would do the job. After he had been reelected, some of the members, including Rankin, met in a House restaurant over the coffee cups to tell stories of their campaigns. Everyone realized that someone was going to ask Rankin a question just to find out how he would respond. Pretty soon one of the members asked him what he had ever done to Mrs. Roosevelt or said about her to cause her to make the statement she did.

John looked very innocent and said, "I don't have the least idea. I never said anything about her or did anything to her that would prejudice her against me." Then he paused for a minute and said, "I did say one time that Mrs. Roosevelt had done this country more harm than any woman had ever done any country except Cleopatra, and that if she had been as good looking as Cleopatra she would have ruined the Republic. She might not have liked that." Everyone roared; they had what they expected — a vivid reply from John Rankin.

The Farmers' Share of the Tariff

One of my most gratifying accomplishments was Section 32 of the Act to Amend the Agricultural Adjustment Act, approved August 24, 1935.

I had for many years tried to find a way to restore to the surplus producing farmer an offset to the tariff, in which he could have no part. Finally I penciled out at my desk a simple bill that authorized an appropriation at the beginning of each fiscal year a sum equal to thirty percent of tariff collections for the previous calendar year to be used by the Secretary of Agriculture to pay any losses on the marketing and distribution of surplus farm commodities. It became Section 32 of a bill with many other provisions. The House passed it unanimously, but the Senate rejected it, I think largely because no one explained it.

We went to conference. When Section 32 was reached Senator John Bankhead said, "That provision is controversial. Let's pass it over and take up the extension of the Bankhead Cotton Tax Act." I said, "No, I'm not sure I'm for extending that tax another year. It's controversial, too. Let's just take them in order." John glared at me and declared, "You haven't any compromise in your make-up. You want everything just your way."

I said, "I'll make you a proposition. If you'll let me write Section 32 like I want it, I'll agree to the extension of your bill for one year."

He got up, marched back and forth, running his hand through the fringe of his hair. I then said, "What's the matter, John? Haven't you any compromise in your make-up?" He wheeled around and said, "All right, I'll agree."

Then I proceeded to strike out the language, "There is hereby authorized" and inserted instead, "There is hereby appropriated annually," thus making it a permanent provision of law. John said, "You don't want much, do you?" My reply, "Are you going to stand by your compromise?" He said, "That is subject to a point of order in the House."

My reply, "I know that and there are several other provisions that are also subject to a point of order. I'll have to get them waived or get a special rule to cover the problem."

Back in the House I submitted the Conference Report and asked that all points of order be waived. Bert Snell, the Minority Floor Leader, asked what the idea was. I related all the steps we had been through, pointed out it was an unanimous report of the Conference Committee, and I told him he wanted to pass the bill, even if we had to get a special rule. He asked if Clifford Hope signed the Conference Report. I said, "Yes, he signed it; all conferees signed it; it is an unanimous report." Snell made no further objection, and the bill passed.

The new law was referred by the President to Secretary of Treasury Henry Morgenthau for comment. When he discovered the Section 32 appropriation, he called me up and vigorously protested. I chided him by telling him he used to be a pretty good farmer, but he got hardening of the financial arteries when he became Secretary of Treasury. He did not think that was funny. He told me he was going to ask the President to veto it. I told him to go ahead, but he had better point out to the President that he would have to veto the whole bill, and we had more things in there that the President wanted than anybody would dream about. That did it. He blew up and said, "Well, then, take the whole blankety-blank Treasury." "No," I said, "we only want our share." But Morgenthau was not one to give up. He got the President to recommend its repeal in the next budget message. A short time after that I had a date with the President and he asked me about the provision I had cooked up to turn $140,000,000 a year over to Henry Wallace to spend. I told him the farmers had been bearing the burden of the tariff for a hundred years without any corresponding benefits, and this provision was not giving them a subsidy, it was simply making partial restitution.

I quoted Alexander Hamilton as saying the tariff would not benefit the farmer and there should be a bounty or set-off paid directly to the farmer either on his production or the manufacture for exportation, to bring things into balance. Those interested secured the enactment of one wing of Hamilton's recommendation, and left out the other wing, the farmer's part. Thus, through these years it has been lopsided. I said I didn't believe in the philosophy of Alexander Hamilton, but he was intellectually honest, and it was from his report that I got my idea.

President Roosevelt said, "That is not a bad idea, is it?" I said "No, it is a good idea." And the President became as enthusiastic as anybody else — and then the critics did not have a chance. They never were able to touch it. From all reports it has served its purpose wonderfully. It was used to start the school lunch program, although that program has outgrown the fund. However, it has been very helpful in many emergencies, especially in disposing of surpluses.

Chapter XIX

THE FRAZIER-LEMKE BILL AND INVALIDATION OF AAA

WHEN SPEAKER RAINEY died in August 1934, Joseph W. Byrns of Tennessee, John McDuffie of Alabama and John Rankin of Mississippi announced their candidacy for Speaker. Claude Fuller of Arkansas, Sam Rayburn, and I announced for Democratic Floor Leader. Fuller and Byrns were supported largely by the same members and were running as a team. Mr. Rayburn came to me and said that if he and I both ran neither of us could be elected; he said if I would withdraw this time that, if he were not chosen, he would stay out of the next opening for leader and support me. Realizing that he was probably right, I agreed to withdraw, although I felt at the time that I had the lead between the two of us. At any rate he was my senior in service.

McDuffie and Rayburn then ran as a team. During the Roosevelt Administration, the vote in the Democratic Conference meant the election; Byrns won handily over McDuffie. At this point Cliff Woodrum, a supporter of McDuffie and Rayburn, moved, apparently with Rayburn's consent, that the conference endorse for the position of leader Will Bankhead of Alabama, Chairman of the Rules Committee, who was in the hospital with a mild heart attack. Woodrum was a beautiful speaker; he referred to Mr. Bankhead as "the uncrowned leader" of the House. Bankhead was chosen, and he served as leader until the death of Speaker Byrns from a heart attack about two years later.

The Frazier-Lemke Bill

By the early part of 1936 the Farm Credit Administration had done a remarkable job. It had refinanced a million farm mortgages and had made many thousands of loans to farmers' cooperative organizations and to livestock producers. In addition, about a half million crop loans were made to finance the year-to-year production of crops. Interest rates paid by farmers over the entire country had been reduced by an average of nearly 40 percent. The four major branches had operated at no cost to the government. The government had advanced $200,000,000 to start the agency, but this sum was being rapidly repaid with interest. Ultimately it was all repaid.

Senator Lynn Frazier and Representative William Lemke, both of North Dakota, introduced a bill which provided for another method of farm financing. Basically, it provided that the Federal Reserve Board would, after an appraisal of normal value of the farm, issue United States currency to the farmer to the full value of the farm, in exchange for a mortgage on the farm. The owner who would pay an administrative cost of 1½ percent interest per annum until the time fixed for repayment of the mortgage. There was no other security for the repayment and no other charge. The measure was referred to the Committee on Agriculture, which did not report it.

The proponents filed a petition to discharge the committee, and bring the bill before the House for action. Under House rules, a petition to discharge a committee, when signed by a majority of the members, may be called up by any member at any time for a record vote. If a majority of the members vote for the motion, the committee is discharged and the bill is placed on the calendar with a privileged status, and it remains the business before the House until a final vote on its passage.

No one expected a majority to sign the motion to discharge, but a vigorous campaign was carried on throughout the country. Telegrams and letters flowed in to the members. As the signatures approached the requisite number, the drive in support of the Frazier-Lemke bill increased. Some who had signed, thinking the necessary 218 signatures could not be reached, removed their names, but 218 finally signed, and the measure was brought up. The Speaker, the floor leader and the head of the Farm Credit Administration asked me to lead the fight against the bill. It was not an easy assignment, but it had to be done in the basic interests of agriculture. The task was more difficult because a number of my close friends favored the bill.

This motion was called up May 13, 1936. In presenting the motion, Mr. Lemke attacked practically everything that either party had ever done, the farm program, the Farm Credit Administration, the Federal Reserve System, and practically our whole philosophy of government.

During the debate I showed that the Farm Credit Administration was furnishing all phases of agriculture lower interest rates than those prevailing in any other country and the lowest rate in this country. I estimated that if the bill passed the House it would very likely not pass the Senate, and if it did the President would veto it. I declared that it would jeopardize the Farm Credit Administration, the nation's first complete and separate credit structure for agriculture. Those of us who carried on the fight for agriculture faced two obstacles: first, those who did not want to do anything, and second, those who wanted to do too much, and by claiming too much to lose the substance of what we already had.

I told the story of the dog in Aesop's fable which crossed a foot bridge with a good piece of meat in his mouth. He saw reflected in the water what he thought was a better piece of meat; turning loose the piece in his mouth, he grasped for the other and thus wound up with nothing. The moral of the fable was: "Beware, lest in grasping at the shadow you lose the substance." That moral, I said, was just as true today as it was 2600 years ago.

The debate was vigorous. Many extreme statements were made. Some of the proponents attacked nearly everything the administration had done for the farmer. I think these extreme attacks hurt their cause. At any rate, the motion was defeated decisively and was not brought up again. It has been my experience that the members of the House will vote right when they know the facts.

Speaker Byrns' Death

Speaker Byrns suffered a heart attack and died on June 4, 1936. It was apparent that Mr. Bankhead, who had been a popular leader, would be chosen Speaker. Mr. Rayburn was visiting in Texas at the time. I received a telegram from him asking that I refrain from making any move until his train got to Washington. When he arrived I told him that I had seriously considered running for leader, that I had slept over the matter and had decided that I would not run, and that I would release him from his promise. He seemed highly pleased; there is not the slightest doubt that Sam Rayburn would have kept his promise. He was that kind of a man. We had been friends since college days, and remained close friends until his death.

I did not tell my friends about my agreement with Mr. Rayburn, in order that he might have a free hand and be elected. Many of my friends were quite sure I would have won. I have never regretted my choice. All my life I had wanted to serve as a United States judge. I was promised and later received the appointment I wanted.

The AAA Invalidated

The question of the constitutionality of the Agricultural Adjustment Act (AAA) came before the Supreme Court in the fall of 1935. Stanley F. Reed, Solicitor General and later Supreme Court Justice, asked me to argue the case before the Supreme Court. I wanted very much to do so, but the Congress had been in almost continuous session since December 1932, and I felt I must spend some time in my home state among the people who had honored me. Mr. Reed then asked that I look over the briefs, which were then ready for printing. The briefs were exceedingly well prepared, and I made only a few minor suggestions.

I was talking with President Roosevelt in his office at noon, January 6, 1936, when Marvin McIntyre, one of the President's secretaries, brought in a teletype message stating that the Supreme Court had just declared the Agricultural Adjustment Act unconstitutional by a 5-to-3 majority, and that Justice Roberts was reading the opinion. The President said he would like Attorney General Homer Cummings, AAA Administrator Chester Davis, Secretary Wallace, Senator Smith and me to get copies of the opinion and of Justice Stone's dissenting opinion and come to his office at 3 o'clock that afternoon for a conference.

The group assembled on schedule. The President read the

opinion to us and the Attorney General read the dissenting opinion. We all agreed that the dissenting opinion was the stronger. The majority opinion was based upon the idea that farming was a local business, and that the Congress had no jurisdiction or authority to control local production. Justice Stone placed the dissent — Justices Brandeis and Cardoza joining — primarily on the constitutional authority of the Congress to regulate commerce. As a matter of fact, the processing fee was levied on the processing for market. More than three-fourths of the processed articles made from the basic farm commodities flowed immediately into interstate and foreign channels. In practical operation, the tax was not collected until 90 to 180 days after processing so that the processor would have an opportunity to sell the processed article before the fee was actually paid. Thus the fee or tax was primarily a method of regulating interstate commerce. The law stipulated that all these taxes should be paid into the general funds of the Treasury, and appropriations were made from the Treasury to carry out the purposes of the Act.

Justice Stone called attention to the fact that "Congress through the Interstate Commerce Commission set aside intra-state railroad rates. It has vitally affected intra-state industries by raising or lowering tariffs. These results are said to be permissible because they are incidents of commerce power and the power to levy duties on imports." The commerce regulatory features were emphasized by this delay in collecting the processing taxes. When the processors sold their goods the taxes would be passed on through channels before ultimate payment by the consumer.

When these taxes were held invalid, the processors already had in their hands some $200,000,000 derived from the taxes collected. I introduced legislation forbidding a refund of any processing taxes unless the processor could show that he had not passed them on to the purchaser in the form of increased prices or back to the producer in the form of decreased prices. In the event he could show that he had paid the tax and had not passed it on, he would be permitted to recover. The funds already collected would be impounded for proper disposition.

The Secretary of Agriculture Henry Wallace inveighed against processors for undertaking to keep these funds, to which in all fairness they were not entitled. Unfortunately, he said that to permit the processors to retain these funds would be "the greatest legalized steal in history." Congressman Treadway of Massachusetts, who had previously attacked Wallace and denounced him on the floor of the House, reiterated his earlier statement that Wallace should be impeached.

I charged Treadway with throwing up a smoke screen to obscure the real issue: what to do with the money which the processors now had and which they had collected from dealers and consumers. I read a letter I had received from the corn refining industry, consisting of ten companies, stating that they "flatly refused to profit by any funds collected and in their hands pursuant to a tax that had been invalidated by the decision of the Supreme Court"; they felt that if they kept the money, they would be "unjustly enriched"; they pledged to refund the money when the proper legal way of doing so was clearly determined.

I stated that the Supreme Court had acted and that we had accepted their decision. I attempted to explain away Mr. Wallace's impulsive remarks made under trying circumstances and argued that talk of impeachment for one unfortunate sentence could not be taken seriously. Then I urged that we address ourselves to the main issue: if the processing tax has been passed on to the consumer or charged back to the producer, should the processor be allowed to keep the money? The essential legislation which I had introduced was later passed, and the entire matter was worked out in a reasonable way.

At the time of the final decision invalidating the Agricultural Adjustment Act, many of the major crops had been planted, the farmers had done their contouring, furrowing, cover-cropping, and strip planting, all under authorized contracts with the Department of Agriculture, as authorized by the AAA. Now there was no money to pay them for all these operations. I was asked by the Department to get an appropriation of $196,000,000 to pay the farmers. The deficiency appropriations bill had already been reported to the House and was on the calendar. All I could do was try.

Mr. Buchanan, Chairman of the Appropriations Committee was already on the floor of the House at about fifteen minutes before noon when Congress was to meet. I told him the situation. I said I wanted to offer an amendment on the floor for an additional $196,000,000, even though it was subject to a point of order. Buchanan told me to explain the problem to John Taber, the ranking Republican on the Committee. He said Taber guarded the Treasury like a hawk, but he was fair, and the House had confidence in him.

I presented the problem to Mr. Taber, and he agreed the farmers should be paid. He asked how much it would take. He whistled when I told him $196,000,000, and said, "That's a lot of money." I said, "Yes, but there are a lot of farmers, and this is a big country."

Taber told me he would probably ask a few questions, but he did not think he would object. It went as we had agreed; I offered the amendment and he asked a number of questions and then said he had no objections. The amendment was adopted. Any one member could have knocked it out by making a point of order. There had been no budget approval, no hearings, and no legislative authorization; and yet no objection was made and the $196,000,000 went through promptly with the deficiency bill. I had long been an admirer of John Taber, but after that I appreciated his fairness even more. He was a hard fighter and questioned all appropriations, but he always did right as he saw it.

The farmers of America were greatly disturbed by the decision of the Supreme Court invalidating the AAA. They organized a march on Washington, led by a farmer named Day from Plainview, Texas. Three thousand farmers came from all over the United States. President Roosevelt invited them to come to the White House grounds. He invited the chairmen and ranking members of the Senate and House Agriculture Committees to attend. The President addressed them with a captivating speech. He told them he had us all working on both temporary and permanent programs, and that we would be glad to listen to their suggestions. The crowd responded with great enthusiasm.

A newspaper man at a conference asked why we could not use the Soil Conservation Act which Jack Dempsey and I had prepared in 1935, as a basis for the payments to farmers. It seemed a happy suggestion. We drafted a bill for enlarging the payments, increasing the soil practices and carrying on the same type of programs that had theretofore been conducted under the invalidated law. There was no difficulty in securing passage. It served the needs very successfully until the permanent, more comprehensive "Soil Conservation and Domestic Allotment Act" passed in 1938. The temporary act did not repeal the 1935 Soil Conservation Act, which is still operating as a permanent soil measure. The Agency established by the 1935 Act has done and is doing wonderful work in conserving, rebuilding, and maintaining the productive soil of our nation.

The Mississippi River System

The Mississippi River system is one of the greatest in the world. According to the Army Engineers' reports, the system includes 2,000 miles of navigable waters. Its approximately 8,000 tributaries stretch all the way from the Allegheny Mountains to the Rocky Mountains and drain parts of 31 states and portions of two provinces of Canada. All these waters flow together and eventually reach the Gulf through one major channel. It is little wonder that at flood time the lower Mississippi becomes a restless river, terrible in its destructive power.

Had the country never been settled, had Nature's policies never been interfered with, the Mississippi River system would probably have never been a serious problem. But, since the ax first rang in the wilderness of America, man has undertaken to harness the wild forces of nature and bend them to his own use. Watersheds in many instances have been stripped of trees, land has been plowed, and erosion has taken place. All of these things have contributed to the flooding of the lower Mississippi; one difficulty was that the bed of the stream was gradually built up until in many places it was higher than the adjacent land. This made necessary the building of higher levees.

As early as 1925, Congressman W. G. Sears of Nebraska and I began to urge a change in policy. We argued that as long as we simply built levees on the lower part of the stream, the protection, while essential, would be temporary. We repeatedly urged that the best way to handle the situation was to go up to the head of the Mississippi, the Missouri and the Ohio Rivers and their tributaries and build check dams and ponds. We further argued that furrowing, chisel-plowing, cover-cropping, contour-furrowing, and soil-building practices would use much of the water where it fell, and floods on the lower Mississippi would thus be greatly reduced. Certainly in the long run it would cost less than the exclusive use of the levy system.

Congressman Sears retired from Congress in 1931, but I continued the fight with the tremendous help of other members and officials of the Department of Agriculture. I insisted on writing such soil conservation practices into practically all farm bills. These practices have all aided in making the Mississippi River Valley one of the great bread-baskets of the world.

Chapter XX

1936 ELECTION—PUMP PRIMING —TENANT FARMERS

The last of the full-time reunions of the Confederate veterans was scheduled to meet in Amarillo in 1936. I asked the Congress for an appropriation of $10,000 to pay expenses for the United States Marine Band to attend and furnish music for the occasion. The band had previously been sent only to official meetings; I argued that the old harsh feelings had largely passed away and that the descendants of the soldiers on both sides had fought heroically side by side in two wars since that time. I urged that this would be a beautiful gesture to the heroes of the "Lost Cause" and further that it would tend to unify the entire country.

The Congress passed the authorizing legislation, and this was followed by including in the last deficiency appropriation bill the funds necessary for the trip. The last day of the session Senator Huey Long of Louisiana filibustered until midnight and Vice President John Garner refused to turn back the clock and declared the Congress adjourned, *sine die*. Final action on the deficiency bill was thus killed.

Several members the next morning expressed sympathy at the loss of the appropriation for the band's trip. I replied that I was still working on it. Captain Branson, the director of the band, called to say all the members of the band were disappointed. I asked the Acting Secretary of the Navy if he could send the band anyway, but he had no funds available. Then I called the passenger traffic manager of the Chesapeake & Ohio Railway, who had arranged the trip with the different companies, and asked why the railways could not send them on the cuff, since we would get the appropriation when Congress met early in January. He said he would call me back in a little while.

Within thirty minutes he walked into my office smiling and said the railways would go ahead with the plan on my assurance that we would make every effort to secure payment in the early part of the next session. He did say, however, that, although they would keep the Pullman cars at Amarillo for the band to sleep in, they could not furnish meals for the seventy-five members for the four days, an estimated tab of about $900. I told him I would personally underwrite that amount, and if the Amarillo Chamber of Commerce would not pay the amount, I would myself.

My friend J. P. Buchanan, the Chairman of the Appropriations Committee, assured me that he would include the appropriation in January if I could get the President to authorize the trip. I told him I planned to ask the President to approve it. He said he had a date to see the President in about thirty minutes, and he would talk to him about it in my behalf. In about an hour the Chairman reported that FDR had hesitated and then approved the trip. Buchanan said he told the President, "You wouldn't do that for anyone except Marvin Jones." The President laughed and said, "Maybe not, but we'll do it. It will create good feeling anyway."

The band made the trip. People came for hundreds of miles to hear it. The band was so pleased that it marched and played almost continuously on the meeting grounds, up and down the street in front of the hotel, and almost everywhere. The people would line the streets and cheer. On the last night, at the Tri-State Fair Grounds, each of the members was presented with a Texas hat, which they wore while playing. For years afterward members of the band would stop me and tell me what a wonderful trip they had to Amarillo.

The 1936 Western Headquarters

In previous campaigns the Republican Party had carried most of the Western states. In 1936, the Democratic National Committee under Jim Farley was very hopeful of carrying those Western states because of our good record in farm programs. The regular Democratic headquarters was in New York, but this year it was decided to establish an additional headquarters in Chicago, and, because of my abiding interest in agriculture, I was put in joint charge of that office with a Mr. Settle, who was head of the party in Indiana.

Mr. Settle spent a great deal of his time in Indiana, but we had the valuable help of Paul Porter, a very talented writer and a good speaker. He spent much time in the headquarters preparing leaflets. We agreed that people in the main do not read long political treatises; we decided therefore that we would get out two-page leaflets on each particular subject, with just a few crisp sentences describing the legislation and how it was voted.

These leaflets proved very popular. We had one on corn, and one each on wheat, cotton, hogs, and other important commodities and subjects. We had a skilled cartoonist who would draw little pictures. Each seperate leaflet told the price of the specific commodity before the passage of farm legislation and the price afterwards. We told the vote in the Congress on the legislation which established the program. This story was told in a few brief sentences. It was easy to determine that if the Republicans had been in charge the program would have been defeated. We asked the simple question, "Do you want the program repealed?" We did the same thing with farm credit legislation, rural electrification, and the marketing agreements for producers of dairy products and other perishable commodities.

The leaflets formed into an almost perfect pattern. For example, the one on rural electrification showed that when that program started only 5 percent of American farms had electricity, but by that time nearly 70 percent had it. We had a "Before and After" cartoon showing one woman using an old-fashioned scrubboard to wash clothes and another using an electric washer. Then came the question, "Do you want this legislation repealed?" And in this as in most other instances, a majority of the Republicans had voted against the measure.

In my speaking tours over the different states, the Democratic headquarters people in the localities would frequently say they wanted five or ten or twenty thousand of the leaflets on wheat, or corn, or whatever it was they were interested in. They much preferred our leaflets to the speeches and long statements that came out of the New York headquarters. People would read our little leaflets and carry them around in their pockets. We sent out 36 million of these leaflets, mostly on request.

Although all those familiar with the situation believed that our astonishing victory in the election was due mainly to the fine work of the Roosevelt administration, we felt it was due in some measure at least to the members of the House and Senate and other talented speakers we sent out from the Western headquarters. Never before had a Democratic triumph been so one-sided. We had letters from the President and from the Chairman of the Democratic National Committee complimenting us upon the way the program was handled in the Western headquarters.

Priming the Pump: Small Lakes

In the Spring of 1937, the economy had slowed a little. The President recommended an appropriation of $4,880,000 to construct a gigantic public works program, to stimulate business and relieve unemployment. The bill contained only a few lines, but it authorized the largest public works program in the Nation's history. The administration was to select the projects covering the entire country.

I called on the Director of Irrigation and Reclamation Division of the Interior Department, to urge the great need in the seventeen Western states between the Mississippi and the Rockies for a small lakes program, to be developed by building small dams on tributary streams. He stated his plans called for huge dams rather than these smaller projects. I tried to argue with him but I soon saw, as he grew more impatient, although he was not really discourteous, that I was not likely to convince him.

When the huge appropriation measure came up in the House, those in charge resisted all amendments, for fear that amendments ear-marking funds would hamper the program. Joe Starnes, a member of the Rivers and Harbors Committee, and I compared notes; he wanted $20,000,000 of the fund for rivers and harbors, and I wanted $10,000,000 for small lakes on tributary streams in the Western states. We agreed that he woud offer his amendment and then I would offer mine as an amendment to his. Then after my amendment was joined to his, supporters of both would win or lose together and would thus hold, in opposition to the bill's managers.

We did as we had planned, and, to the surprise of those in charge of the bill, both amendments were adopted. The bill's managers were disturbed; they moved adjournment over the weekend and consulted the President. They came to Starnes and me to say that if we would withdraw our amendments the President would assure us he would allot a substantial amount of the funds for the purposes we wanted to serve. We knew that our amendments might be lost in the Senate or in conference, or that they might be swamped in a multitude of other amendments that might be offered if they were left in the bill. So we agreed to the proposition and withdrew our amendments.

This is how the small lakes program was started for the Western states. I followed this with a bill to authorize a continuance of the program. Six were placed in the Panhandle-Plains area of Texas and many throughout the West. They have been invaluable. Secretary Ickes asked me why that program was placed in Agriculture. I frankly told him about the attitude of the head of his division on irrigation and reclamation. Shortly thereafter he transferred the man in charge of that division to another position. Later on Secretary Ickes arranged with Senator Francis Case of North Dakota to introduce a bill authorizing the Interior Deparement to continue and expand the work, and I was happy to help in its passage. Altogether it has been a wonderful program.

Home Ownership by Farm Tenants

For several years following 1933, Senator John Bankhead of Alabama and I worked on legislation dealing with the problems of farm tenancy. We wanted a program to permit tenants to purchase farm homes on long-term payments at low interest. I visited with Charles Peary, the president of the bank in the small town near where I was born; we had attended country school together in our boyhood days. I asked him if he could name any tenants in the neighborhood who would pay out a farm home if permitted to purchase it on 30 years' time at 3½ percent annual interest. He promptly replied that he could name tenants who would work their hearts out if given such a chance. Then I asked if there were any who would not succeed, and he replied that he could name tenants who, if given a farm paid for and well stocked, would lose it within 5 years. I asked him to write down the names of five tenant farmers he thought would succeed. Then I made the same request of the general merchant, Jess Leazer. Four of the five names were on both lists.

Back in Washington we wrote a provision in the bill that there should be a county committee in each county, composed of a local banker, a businessman and a farmer. All applications would first go to the local committee; if it approved, the application would go up through channels; if it rejected the application, that would end the matter, with no appeal. With that change we were finally able to get the bill favorably reported to the House.

We had quite a discussion in the House with considerable opposition. The bill passed the House. When it was ready for passage in the Senate one of the Senators moved that the measure be officially named "The Bankhead-Jones Act" and the motion was carried unanimously. Senator McNary of Oregon, the Republican floor leader, commented on the floor of the Senate that this was the first time in the history of the Senate that the authors have been officially named in a bill, but he thought their long-time efforts justified the exception.

The success of the program was overwhelming, surprising even its authors. Many of the farm families buckled down and finished paying off their mortgages long before they were due. The program of home purchasing was self-supporting. All of the money advanced by the government has been, or is being, repaid. A nation of homeowners is a stable country and has a loyal citizenship. Such a nation will endure. The more family homeowners, the stronger the Republic, and the more secure its liberty.

In October 1949, I attended the Texas State Fair at Dallas, where a celebration was held for the Texas tenants who had paid off their mortgages within ten years. Three hundred mortgages were burned that day. Three families stood before the crowd to tell the story of their working together in paying out the farm, raising chickens and livestock and selling milk, butter and eggs. I wished that every member of Congress could have heard these human interest stories. It was like an old-fashioned camp meeting. There was hardly a dry eye in the house as each family told of their struggles to own a home, and how happy they were to call it their own. It was the easiest audience to address in all my long experience. They insisted on presenting me with a fine Stetson hat. I still have it, and I treasure it highly.

Chapter XXI

THE SUGAR ACT

THE JONES-COSTIGAN SUGAR ACT normally would have have been referred to the Ways and Means Committee, because it materially changed the tariff on sugar. I had never taken any special interest in sugar, except to use it in my coffee and on my strawberries, when I could get them. I knew little about it. One day I met in the office of Senator Joseph T. Robinson, the Senate Floor Leader, with about twenty important persons in the government, both in Congress and in the executive branch. Several senators, including Robinson and Ellison D. Smith, and Cordell Hull and others from the executive branch were present.

They said they had found it necessary to have a sugar act. The retail price of sugar was fluctuating from as low as six cents per pound to as high as twenty-seven cents. Conditions were bad in Cuba and in most sugar-producing areas. The administration wanted a sugar act that would allocate the American market among the various sugar-producing areas and stabilize the price of sugar. The great sugar-producing areas were Cuba, Puerto Rico, the western beet growers, the sugar cane areas of Florida and Louisiana, Hawaii, the Philippines, and some cane-producing areas in Michigan and other central states. All of these areas were in trouble, and they all wanted the American market. The administration wanted to reduce the tariff on sugar and they wanted a processing fee collected and the proceeds paid to the producers in this country who accepted their allocated portion of the American market.

It developed that they wanted me to handle the legislation. I protested that I was completely swamped with work, but they insisted. I said my people were not interested in anything except having a stabilized retail price for sugar. I was doubtful about putting a processing fee on sugar when there was a plentiful offshore supply. Someone suggested they were going to reduce the tariff on sugar by the amount of the processing fee.

I said if I should handle the legislation, I would want it written into the legislation that the processing fee should never be more than the amount of the reduction of the tariff, so it would not increase the cost of sugar for the consumer. I remember that Mr. Tugwell was there and he said, "Oh, we can't do that." I said, "We can do it, and it will be done if I handle the legislation." Cordell Hull and Senator Robinson said they did not see any reason why it should not be written into the legislation.

Then I made another suggestion. I thought, if we had an allocation of the American market among the different sugar-producing areas, that, as a condition to their securing that allotment, the offshore areas should be required to have a six-months' reserve supply on hand at all times to avoid a sugar shortage. The official group agreed to that change.

The discussion had taken all morning. Senator Robinson had to leave, and the meeting broke up without my agreeing to handle the bill. About 2 o'clock President Roosevelt telephoned me to say he wanted me to handle the sugar legislation. I told him it really belonged to the Ways and Means Committee. He said, "Well, the situation is desperate and we need quick action. There is danger of riots in Cuba and elsewhere. The Ways and Means Committee will probably take months in hearings. You have a habit of getting quick action. And as a special favor to me I want you to handle the legislation." Of course I had to do it.

I had to learn about sugar. I called in some experts, dropped everything else, and spent two or three days going over the matter with men who had spent a lifetime in sugar. All domestically produced sugar and much of that grown elsewhere was refined in this country. There were refineries along the Atlantic seaboard and two or three in California that further refined sugar produced overseas.

We had quite a fight in the committee on the sugar act. One member of the committee, Fred Cummings from Colorado, and one or two others from other sugar-producing areas did not like the limitation that would be placed upon their part of the market. The men who came up from the Department of Agriculture to the first hearings before the Committee on Agriculture were not fully familiar with the text of the bill and not experienced in testifying before the Committee. We adjourned that hearing, and at the next hearing the Department of Agriculture and the State Department sent men who could do the job more effectively. I think they had thought the measure would just slip through without any trouble. They showed the whole purpose was to help solve the problem and to make it possible for sugar producers in this country to continue to produce in a stable market without increasing the price to the consumer.

After a rather extended hearing of two or three days, the Committee reported the bill. Most of those in the domestic sugar-producing areas became convinced from the discussion and from the evidence that stabilized production and prices were for the interest of all.

We finally passed the bill through the House. In the Senate it was handled by Senator Edward P. Costigan, a very wonderful man, a very fair man. He thoroughly understood the whole sugar question; I do not know of anyone who knew as much about sugar as he did. He was very helpful to me all the way through to the final passage of the measure.

The price of sugar was stabilized after the Sugar Act was put into effect. It was enacted for a definite period and was extended from time to time by resolution or by reenactment, with necessary changes. For the first five years the act was in operation, the average retail price of sugar was so stable and so low that consumer complaints dwindled to zero. We did not hear any complaints about the price of sugar except during wartime when there was a sugar shortage. The act worked out beautifully.

Of course there was a continuous struggle, then and later, by the different sugar-producing areas to get a higher allotment for their share of the market. As the act came up for renewal, Senator Joseph C. O'Mahoney asked my advice on how to proceed. I suggested a resolution extending the act for another period. I even dictated to my secretary a resolution to extend the Sugar Act, and this was the resolution that passed the Congress.

Chapter XXII

AN ALL-INCLUSIVE NEW FARM BILL

IN 1937 THE AGRICULTURE COMMITTEE, the farm organizations and the Department of Agriculture began working on long-range farm bills. The Department and one of the farm organizations — The American Farm Bureau Federation — agreed on a measure that had compulsory production controls enforced by heavy penalties against non-complying farmers, plus sufficient appropriations to give farmers much higher prices for their reduced production. It made no reference to preservation of export markets, although it would have affected them vitally. The House Agriculture Committee felt that the bill was unworkable, would destroy the foreign markets, and was of doubtful constitutionality. The Committee also wanted several new features not in the proposed bill. I was authorized to draft a bill that embodied the Committee's position and to add any new features that I thought desirable, and I did so.

The Department and the farm organization started a tremendous propaganda drive for their compulsory bill. The organization called a meeting in Amarillo, and invited all the county committeemen and county agents in my district. The meeting was attended by 3,000 people, mostly farmers and farm officials. It was explained that they were trying to get me to sponsor their proposed bill. I was not even notified of the meeting. Some of those present asked why I was not invited. There was quite a discussion. I received several letters from friends later on saying they would not have attended if they had known what was up; others said they would leave the whole matter to my judgment.

About that same time, Speaker Will Bankhead asked Floor Leader Sam Rayburn and me to meet with Secretary Wallace to discuss the proposed bill. The Speaker asked me to explain my position. I told him that I felt the proposed bill was unworkable, that I had the draft of a much better bill practically completed, which the Committee preferred. Mr. Wallace replied that two Senators had already introduced their bill, and he thought it would pass the Senate. The Speaker then wanted to know what I would do if the Senate passed it. I said I would have no choice but to fight it to the end; that the Supreme Court had already invalidated one compulsory bill; and that I did not propose to go down that same alley again. The Speaker then said, "Mr. Secretary, there is no use. No bill can be passed without the Chairman's approval. The House has complete confidence in him. You should change your bill to comply with his wishes."

They did not give up. They persuaded a member of the Congress to call a meeting of other members in another committee room. Again I was not notified, but a friend told me about the meeting while it was in session. I immediately went to the meeting. I told them I was that day introducing a Committee bill which had many new features, and that at least they should see it before taking any position. The meeting broke up without action. I made a speech on the floor of the House, telling all about the Amarillo meeting which was called without notifying me, and about the other pressure activities, and that it was apparently a high pressure movement in an effort to whip me into line; that they had picked the wrong man; that I had always been frank with the House and that I asked the members to read and compare the two bills. When I had finished I was given a rising demonstration of approval in which both sides joined.

Some desirable provisions in our bill not in the Senate bill were: (1) an authorized $10,000,000 appropriation to establish research laboratories in major farm regions, to study new uses and markets for farm commodities; (2) a graduated scale of payments to complying farmers, with a gradually reducing rate in the upper brackets and a top payment of $10,000, on any one farm; (3) a program protecting tenants from removal by landlords to deprive them of their current compliance payment share; and (4) a provision authorizing the Secretary of Agriculture to intervene in any transportation rate hearing to prevent a disadvantage to farmers. We relied mainly on voluntary compliance, with a penalty only for exceeding the market quota. The payments were closely linked to soil conserving and soil building crops and practices.

It was a spirited and interesting fight, but the House bill passed by 242 to 157. Our bill was sent back to the Senate while their bill was still pending. The Senate struck out all after the enacting clause of the House measure and inserted their bill as a substitute. The only substantial change made in their bill was to offer on the floor of the Senate a research provision exactly like the one included in the House bill, except for a reduced amount.

The entire bill was thus thrown into conference. We spent a month in conference with ten Senators and five members of the House. Senator Smith of South Carolina presided. He was one of the most interesting men in public life and he gloried in his nickname of "Cotton Ed." During the Roosevelt years, he was chairman of the Committee on Agriculture in the Senate while I had the comparable position in the House.

The bills as passed by the two houses were based on different philosophies, and it was thus a wide-ranging conference. We stayed in a good humor most of the time, but sometimes toward the end of a long day we would tire and tempers would flare. At one point when Senator Smith lost a point, he threw down his papers and stalked out, leaving his seat vacant. Someone suggested I take the chair. I said, "No, let's leave it vacant and go right along as if nothing has happened. He'll be back in five minutes. I have sat with him in many conferences and like most of us he blows up occasionally." In less than five minutes he slowly walked back and took his seat. I called his attention to the matter under discussion, he made a statement; we agreed, and the conference moved right along.

Several days later, toward the close of the conference, we were all a little tired, and I could see the Senator was about to blow up again. I interrupted the meeting to ask him to retell a campaign story I had once heard him tell. He seemed delighted. Here is the story as I recall it. He was opposed in South Carolina by a man named Harris, a noted lawyer and a very fine speaker. He attacked Senator Smith's record along many lines, charging, among other things, that Senator Smith had many members of his family on the government payroll; he capped the catalog of relatives with an 80-

year-old aunt who was unable to do anything except wind up the clock and put out the cat at night. South Carolina law requires every candidate, state and federal, to meet his opponent face-to-face during the last month of the campaign at least once in every county. On one such occasion Mr. Harris brought down the house with his story about the old aunt.

Senator Smith responded that he had served in the Senate for thirty years and that his record was an open book. He ignored all of Harris's charges except the one about the old 80-year-old aunt. As for that charge, "That's not true. She is 83 years old and that old lady, that saintly mother, reared me as an orphan boy and through these years she has been the inspiration for the greatest United States Senator you folks ever had. Of course, she is on the payroll and she will be there so long as I am in the United States Senate." The people, with that answer, seemed to forget the other charges. The whole conference group enjoyed the Senator's recital, and soon the group's work was moving right along.

The conferees retained practically all the provisions of the House bill; many of the Senators liked the House bill better than their own. We reported the measure as H.R. 8505, its original number. It was adopted by both bodies and signed by the President in early 1938. Its operation was a great success. Ed O'Neal, the President of the farm organization that had sponsored the Senate bill, told me a year later that the bill had worked wonderfully and his organization liked both the new provisions and the over-all result. I appreciated his compliment. Ed O'Neal had a heart interest in the American farmer and he was a real man.

Chapter XXIII

HARVARD UNIVERSITY STUDIES NEW FARM BILL

 IN 1939, THE LITTAUER GRADUATE SCHOOL of Government at Harvard University spent an entire term on the subject of "The Processes of Enacting Legislation." The class was made up largely of young men already in government, who were taking a year's leave of absence on scholarship. Their basis of study for the full term was "The Agricultural Act of 1938." I was requested by Dr. Froelich, the Director of the School, to address the class, which met at four in the afternoon; it consisted of about fifty eager and alert young men and five older men. I was told I should make a twenty-minute statement to be followed by a full question and answer session.

 I soon found that these young men had read and studied every line of the extensive House Committee hearings and the shorter Senate hearings. If I had not lived with that bill since its inception, I might have had some difficulty. They would run along with innocuous questions and then suddenly would ask a stem-winder. They were much interested in what went on in conference, since they found no record of those proceedings. I explained that we took up the paragraphs in each bill one by one, discussing the differences in wording, purpose and effect; sometimes we would compromise, using a part of both provisions, sometimes we would agree on one or the other as written, and at other times we would write an entirely new provision, trying always to stay within the framework of the two bills.

 One student asked, "There were ten Senators in the conference and only five members of the House, and yet the bill as reported by the conference is almost exactly like the House bill. How did you do it?" I told him the number in each conference group made little difference, since the majority of each group had to approve any action. As for our prevailing in the conference, I said Senators are busy men, usually serving on several committees, with some Senators simply preferring the House bill.

Another student asked, "What sort of a legislator is 'Cotton Ed' Smith?" I replied that Senator Smith had served in the Senate thirty years, that he was a most effective public speaker, that his primary interest was cotton and he watched legislation on that subject like a hawk, that he and I had always gotten along together, and that I was very fond of him personally.

Then came another question: "If the Senate bill had been adopted as written, do you think it would have worked?" I replied that it might have worked if we had been under a Hitler government, where one man had authority to dispose of a non-complying farmer, but that I did not think it would have worked successfully in a free country.

Dr. Froelich told me I knew more about this subject than anyone they had found, and the boys did not want to halt the discussion.

The meeting disbanded at 7 o'clock; Dr. Froelich introduced me to the five older men, all of whom were professors; one of them was an exchange professor from a German university; I apologized for the statement I had made about the Hitler government, but Dr. Froelich interrupted to say that the German professor probably felt the same way I did. A group of them took me to dinner and stayed with me until my train left at 10:45, plying me with questions and showing me the university grounds. I had a grand time and was much impressed with these unusual young men.

A few days later Dr. Froelich wrote that I had been selected as one of the trustees of the Littauer Graduate School of Government. I was much impressed with the wide ranging operations of the great Harvard University.

The Coronado Celebration

In July of 1939 the House had under consideration a measure to provide funds to celebrate the explorations of Coronado, who had led a group through several southwestern states in search of the fabulous wealth of the legendary Seven Cities of Cibola. The appropriation was sponsored by representatives of Arizona and New

Mexico but was joined by other congressmen who represented the parts of several southwestern states through which the expedition passed. I was asked to make a speech in favor of the appropriation. I undertook to answer the objection that only a small segment of the country was involved. Except for DeSoto, Coronado perhaps covered more area than any of the early-day explorers. He covered a fabulous area that includes the Grand Canyon, the matchless Carlsbad Caverns, what is said to be the oldest church in the United States, and many other interesting places.

"Man cannot live by bread alone." Neither can a nation. I glory in our material wealth, but the building of a strong people calls for something more than silver and gold. I recall as a boy reading of the hanging of the lantern in the Old North Church as a signal to Paul Revere. I said then I would rather see the Old North Church than anything else in North America, and I have kept that feeling through the years. Later I visited the Old North Church and felt a strong surge of patriotism; that is where the whole thing started. I believe that sentiment, tradition, and history, go far toward building a nation and cementing the lives of a people.

Freight Rate Inequities

During the latter part of my final year of service in the House of Representatives, I was asked to preside during the consideration of a bill affecting freight rates. The measure was reported by the Committee on Interstate and Foreign Commerce. For many years there had been what I considered discrimination against farm and ranch products. I called another member to the Chair and offered an amendment requiring the Commission to correct the discrimination.

I pointed out that iron and steel shipped from Gary, Indiana, to New York take a domestic rate of 52 cents, but an export rate of 36 cents; while cotton or wheat shipped to New Orleans scheduled for export receive no rate reductions. Such reductions encourage export trade, but if it is a good practice for manufactured products, why would it not be good for agricultural products?

The amendment was adopted. The measure was sent to conference with the Senate, and it developed that the only way the Senate conferees would agree to the amendment was to debate the mandatory feature and provide that the Commission would consider removing discrimination whenever it was found practicable to do so. The Chairman of the House conferees told me it appeared that was all we could get, and I reluctantly agreed.

Chapter XXIV

LAST DAYS IN CONGRESS

PRESIDENT FRANKLIN ROOSEVELT appointed me Judge of the United States Court of Claims on April 9, 1940, and I was confirmed by the Senate the next day. The President had told me, before sending my name to the Senate, that he wanted me to continue in the House during the remainder of the year, especially to look out for the agriculture appropriation bill, and I agreed not to take my oath of office until the end of the year.

There were several odds and ends that I needed to finish up before I left the House, including some vitally needed changes in the sugar legislation and the Farm Credit Administration Act. I was especially interested in the appropriation act because it carried the annual appropriation for the Tenant Home Purchasing law which Senator Bankhead and I had sponsored about five years before.

Many people had doubts about this program and about the astonishing immediate success with which it met. It was essential that a staunch friend of the program be present when this item was reached in the annual appropriation bill. I was also very much interested in obtaining an adequate appropriation for water conservation and water supply in the arid areas of the country.

Henry Wallace as Vice President

The Democratic National Convention was held in Chicago in July 1940. The President was nominated for a third term and Henry Wallace was nominated for Vice President. Soon thereafter Speaker William B. Bankhead, who had been Chairman of the Convention, asked me to go to Des Moines, Iowa, and deliver the speech officially notifying Henry Wallace of his nomination. I asked him if it would not be more appropriate for him as Chairman of the Convention to deliver the speech of notification. He told me that he had some important matters to take care of in the House before the planned early adjournment and that he was not in good physical condition. I agreed to go as a personal favor to him.

President Roosevelt asked me to come to the White House and talk to him. He wanted me to go with Wallace on a barnstorming tour across the country starting the second day after the notification in Des Moines. The caravan left Chicago to campaign through Illinois, Missouri, Kansas and Oklahoma, conducting from six to eight meetings a day. When we reached Woodward, Oklahoma, I received a wire that a very important bill would be brought up in the House the next day and that the vote was expected to be close. I left the tour, which went on to California, but I rejoined them as they came back through the midwest.

In December after the election a group of members of the Congress, both the House and the Senate, and a number of other officials were invited to attend the inauguration of Avila Camacho as President of Mexico. The Chairmen of the major committees of both houses of Congress and many other officials and former officials were invited. I went along. Henry Wallace, the newly elected Vice President, was the guest of honor. He brushed up on his Spanish and made several speeches in that language on the trip. That apparently pleased the Mexicans. The gala occasion was celebrated in many ways in Mexico City. The flags were flying, the bands were playing and a series of entertainments went on both day and night. There were parades both before and after the inaugural ceremony. There were many speeches by both Americans and Mexicans. Ambassador Josephus Daniels provided a variety of entertainment. A bull fight was arranged one afternoon and theater and garden parties kept things going all during our stay in Mexico City. After the celebration was over the Vice President-Elect invited me to go with him to a resort on the West Coast of Mexico for a week of relaxation, but I needed to return to Washington to prepare for my work on the United States Court of Claims to begin in January.

Major Bills and Presidential Pens

Perhaps this is an appropriate place to list the major bills I handled during my period of service as Chairman of the Committee on

Agriculture. I have eleven pens with which bills were signed by President Roosevelt, and this was at a time when they did not give such pens away by the bushel; there were only one each to the chairmen of the House and Senate Committees which handled a bill. My pens are on display in the Panhandle Historical Building in Canyon, Texas.

1. The Agriculture Adjustment Act of 1933
2. The Emergency Farm Mortgage Refinancing Act of 1933
3. The Farm Credit Administration Act of 1933
4. The Cattle Purchase Act, to purchase cull cattle and distribute the meat for relief
5. The Resettlement Act, to finance work for unemployed
6. The Soil Conservation and Rebuilding Act
7. The Commodity Exchange Act
8. The Tenant Home Purchase Act
9. The Temporary Farm Act, to replace the farm program invalidated by the Supreme Court
10. The Jones-Costigan Sugar Act
11. The Agricultural Adjustment Act of 1938
12. The Marketing Agreements Act for Perishable Commodities

I also have two additional pens, one given me by President Coolidge with which he signed my bill to conduct research in new uses and new markets for cotton in 1927; and one with which President Hoover signed my bill to establish Regional Agricultural Credit Corporations for loans to livestock producers. I was the author of both these measures. These two pens are also on display in Canyon, Texas.

During the ten peacetime years beginning with 1921 and ending with late 1931 we were in the minority, and during one Congress we were outnumbered more than three to one. Many members felt there was no use to continue to struggle, but I kept on fighting. I do not believe in abandoning principle when you find you are in the minority. There is not a social, political, economic or even religious privilege we enjoy today that was not purchased by the blood and tears and sacrifices of a dedicated minority. A minority has stood in the vanguard of every great movement of the earth and has blazed the path that humanity later beat into a highway of progress.

Leaving the House of Representatives

The decision to leave the House of Representatives was the most difficult of my life. I had entered that body as a young man and had devoted to it the best years of my life. I had made a special study of parliamentary procedure. I had led in securing the passage of more important legislation than any other single member under the Roosevelt New Deal.

I was reluctant to leave the Congress, but there were practical considerations. During the most of my twenty-four years of service, my congressional district of fifty-three counties was settling rapidly. It was difficult to do my work and keep in touch with the new people that were pouring into the district. I was faced with the choice of slighting my work or neglecting my district, and I could bring myself to do neither. I always enjoyed visiting the wonderful citizens of the Panhandle-Plains country; I knew my home would always be there, and it still is.

Chapter XXV

ECONOMIC STABILIZATION

In January 1941 I began my service as a judge of the United States Court of Claims. Some of my former law clerks have selected a number of my opinions that they considered to be of unusual human interest to lawyers and laymen. These have been published in a separate volume entitled *Should Uncle Sam Pay — When and Why?* But we will see more of the Court of Claims later on.

During the year 1941, I kept in touch with agricultural legislation and with the work of the Department as best I could in my spare time. I was called rather frequently, especially during the first few months after I left the Congress.

On December 7, 1941, Pearl Harbor was bombed, many of our air pilots killed, some of our battleships were sunk or destroyed, and many of our planes were wrecked on the ground. There was fear that our West Coast might be bombed, and many feared our country might be invaded. I almost regretted that I had left the Congress.

I realized that if the war lasted for some time, there would be a price control bill, which in World War I was handled by the House Committee on Agriculture. For some reason this time the bill was referred to the Banking and Currency Committee. I would have preferred that the Committee on Agriculture handle the price control legislation, because then the ceiling price of farm products should have been placed at parity in the beginning, and all other ceiling prices would have fitted into the related pattern. This would have saved a great deal of controversy over subsidies, for none would have been needed. The ceiling on wages and industrial prices could then have been geared to the cost-of-living index and readjusted at stated periods.

As it was worked out, the ceiling prices of some farm products were frozen so low that it was necessary to use subsidies, which threw the whole system out of kilter. Of course some subsidies might have been necessary in any event. The only reason for mentioning this here is the possibility that a similar situation may happen again. Later some of my friends in the House suggested that, if I had remained as Chairman of the House Committee on Agriculture, the price legislation would have been handled by that Committee.

In 1942, James F. Byrnes resigned from the Supreme Court to accept appointment as Director of Stabilization, a position established by Executive Order, with authority over practically all departments and agencies of government. He was assigned offices in the east wing of the White House. One evening in November 1942 he phoned me that the President had decided to establish a War Food Administration to control production and distribution of food, and to determine allotments of food to our armed forces, to our allies through Lend-Lease, and for domestic civilian use. The Administrator would have charge of all the active branches of the Department of Agriculture and he would be chairman of the Allied Food Board.

Mr. Byrnes told me the President wanted me to be War Food Administrator. I told him I thought the Secretary of Agriculture should handle that position, or there might be friction. He said the President would like to have me as Secretary of Agriculture anyway. I replied I did not want that position and that I had declined it before. I added that I would be glad to take leave of absence from my judicial position to do any kind of essential war work the President wanted me to do. Mr. Byrnes phoned later to say Claude Wickard would be appointed War Food Administrator, but that the President did not think it would work out well. Mr. Wickard was appointed.

The Texas Delegation in Congress held weekly luncheons in the Speaker's dining room; as an ex-member, I was privileged to attend, which I did about once a month. One day in January 1943 James F. Byrnes spoke at the luncheon, and afterwards he invited me to ride in his car with him, since the Court of Claims was just across the street from the White House. On the way Mr. Byrnes urged that I become his assistant, taking charge of the agricultural and food production and distribution phases of his work. He said laughingly he was anxious for me to join him because I was the only person he had ever known who could work with "Cotton Ed" Smith. I joined him the next day and was given an office in the White House near Mr. Byrnes.

One of my first assignments was to attend a meeting in Washington of the National Cattle Producers, called to discuss putting a price ceiling on live cattle. Mr. Byrnes said the Office of Price Administration wanted the ceiling, but that he was afraid there might be fireworks, and he wanted me to try to avoid trouble. Mr. Byrnes had not made up his mind about a ceiling; I told him I thought it could not be enforced, because no one can tell with any degree of accuracy the quality of the meat until the hide is removed. The packers and livestock men agreed on this point, although they fought about nearly everything else.

The meeting was in a packed auditorium in the Washington Hotel. The atmosphere seemed noisy, restless, and hostile. The suave economist in charge called the meeting to order and began by saying: "I would be less than frank if I did not tell you that we have already decided to place a ceiling on live cattle." Pandemonium broke loose. The meeting was immediately almost totally out of hand.

I arose and took the floor. I told them Mr. Byrnes had the final say in the matter and he had told me a few minutes earlier that the issue had not been determined. He was anxious to have this gathering discuss the question and see whether any practical solution could be arranged. The group quieted down. Most of them knew me from my days in Congress, and they knew we could talk the problem out. It was an earnest discussion, and the cattlemen at least felt they had been given a hearing. The right to be heard is one of the most highly prized rights of a free people. The attorney for the cattle raisers told me afterwards that if I had not spoken up the outraged cattlemen might have manhandled the chairman. I think the economist did not realize what a close call he had.

While there was considerable discussion later among the officials, no ceiling was ever placed on live cattle. The ceiling on meat and meat products apparently held prices in line as well as it was done in other forms of staple food. Naturally the black markets complicated all ceiling price regulation of food products, but the over-all results of the work were surprisingly successful in the long run.

Many exciting questions arose while I served as assistant to James F. Byrnes. In the vast war machine there were innumerable conflicts both among the regular governmental agencies and the war agencies. In resolving these conflicts Mr. Byrnes worked long hours, sometimes far into the night. I greatly admired his alert mind, his ability to grasp essential facts, his courage and his talent for making quick decisions. Next to President Roosevelt, he was the vital spark in the operative end of the war effort. On his able staff advising him, among others, were Ben Cohen, Don Russell, General Marshall, Charles Fahey, frequently Bernard Baruch, and later General Clay.

No freeze order had been issued at the time I became Mr. Byrnes' assistant, but he was trying to hold everything, including wages and prices, as of that date. Otherwise a spiral of inflation would greatly increase the cost of the war. The War Production Board allocated basic materials in short supply, such as rubber, iron, and steel. Many other materials came into short supply later. All manufacturers, distributors, and other groups agreed to the effort to hold the price line, but everyone winced when controls were applied to him. While the problems covered the entire field, I will restrict my discussion to the story of food.

The Secretary of Agriculture, as War Food Administrator, found that some farm commodity prices had been frozen at abnormally low levels and were out of line in relation to other prices. Numerous agents and representatives of farmers objected to the low ceiling prices fixed on different farm commodities. Members of Congress would come to us with letters and telegrams urging adjustments. The Office of Price Administration invariably objected to suggested increases. I would talk with all of them and report to Byrnes, who usually took my recommendation.

Among the group that came to us representing the Department

of Agriculture there were sometimes differences of opinion. In that big sprawling organization there were some ambitious men who slyly undertook to undermine what the Secretary of Agriculture thought had been agreed upon. Perhaps this is natural in any large organization, but it was quite evident here.

One of Claude Wickard's greatest difficulties was that corn and hog prices were out of line. In some central western states, more than 80 per cent of the corn raised never crosses a county line; it is fed right in the county where it is produced. When the ceiling price of corn was agreed upon there had been a large surplus of corn. Prices were now out of line, and the corn producers would not sell. Agriculture urged that the ceiling price of corn be increased but the Office of Price Administration was opposed.

An OPA economist argued in a twelve page thesis to Byrnes that a ten cent per bushel increase in the price of corn would force an increase in chicken, turkey, and other prices that would ultimately cost the consumer two billion dollars. Jimmy Byrnes asked my opinion on the document. In a memorandum of less than two pages I proved his statistics were faulty. In the great corn belt more than 80 percent of corn never crosses a county line. It is fed locally. Less than 20 percent is normally sold in the general market, so an increase of 10 cents per bushel would cost the consumer, in any event, less than one hundred million dollars. But, in fact, since the present ceiling price of corn is relatively less than the price of hogs, cattle and fowls, no corn is being sold at all. Thus an increase of 10 cents would increase the cost to poultry feeders very little, if any, since corn was not moving and poultry feeders were using higher cost feeds of all kinds, including wheat. Despite these facts the OPA continued to oppose any increase in the price of corn.

The voluntary agreement of various groups to hold the line had been undertaken before I was connected with the Byrnes office. I felt that the original bill authorizing these price controls should have provided that no ceiling on a farm commodity could be fixed below parity. For many years the House Committee on Agriculture had fought for a parity price for all farm products. The theory of parity was that for basic farm commodities the purchasing power of the farmer had been ideal between 1909 and 1913. During those years prices of farm commodities were on a basis of equality with the prices of manufactured products. Since that time, surplus production, high tariffs and discriminatory freight rates had all worked to the farmer's disadvantage.

Many controversies between Claude Wickard, the War Food Administrator, and the Office of Price Administration were referred to the Byrnes office for settlement. We had begun to hear complaints of Wickard's methods of operation. Byrnes and his staff, in a separate meeting with the President, decided to remove Wickard as War Food Administrator. Byrnes then held another meeting with Bernard Baruch, Harry Hopkins, General Marshall and several others, to select a new War Food Administrator.

Mr. Byrnes told me they had tentatively agreed to ask me to be War Food Administrator, and that after a few minutes they would probably send for me and ask me to accept that position. In a few minutes I was asked to step into the conference. I went in and spoke up before they could offer me the position and told them I knew the best man in the United States to suggest for the position. He was Chester Davis, President of the Federal Reserve Bank in St. Louis; he had for a number of years been in charge of the Agricultural Adjustment Administration. They thanked me and said they would take my suggestion under consideration, and in a few minutes the meeting broke up.

Mr. Byrnes came to my office smiling; they had unanimously picked me as War Food Administrator and I had talked them out of it before they told me of their decision. They had sent for Chester Davis and asked him to be administrator; he was appointed. Davis came to my office, since he and I had been great friends through the years; I took him in and introduced him to Mr. Byrnes. One of the early changes Davis recommended was to increase the price of corn by 10 to 15 cents a bushel.

Chapter XXVI

THE FIRST INTERNATIONAL FOOD CONFERENCE

JIMMY BYRNES told me that the President wanted to call an international conference on food and agriculture of forty-four nations, including those who were friendly to the allied cause, to meet in Hot Springs, Virginia. President Roosevelt wanted me to head the delegation from the United States and to have charge of the conference. Byrnes advised me to talk first to Secretary of State Cordell Hull and then to the President.

I talked to Secretary Hull and also to Under Secretary Sumner Welles. They outlined to me the general plans. The State Department would take care of planning, and the reception of the delegations and the housing and feeding of the six hundred delegates. There would be a great many experts and representatives from the Department of Agriculture. We then discussed what we felt should be the agenda of the conference. We agreed that a committee would be organized to draft the agenda. After the plans were made, they were submitted to the President, who had already made several suggestions.

I then talked to the President about the conference. He said that after World War I, the allies fell apart immediately and found it difficult to agree on anything. He wanted the food and agriculture representatives from the different nations to meet and see if we could agree on a program while we were still working together. He thought I could come nearer to getting the agreements through than anyone else. He also said I would head the host delegation and that custom decreed that I would be elected President of the Conference. It required about two months to work out the details; the date was set for May 18, 1943.

The President said that at his North African conference with Stalin and Churchill no newsmen were permitted to be present, and afterward they were called in and told what had been agreed upon.

He said it worked out beautifully in wartime, and he wanted the food conference to use the same method. In the absence of publicity the discussion would be freer, the danger of enemy bombing might be reduced and the safety of the foreign delegates could be more easily insured. A body of Marines would guard our building. I could meet with newspaper people who would be housed in an adjoining building, and give them a full account of what had taken place each day.

I told the President that I thought this arrangement would cause difficulty, for American newsmen were accustomed to full access to meetings or at least access to the building. He suggested I take along Mr. McDermott, the State Department publicity man, to brief the newsmen. I still had misgivings, but he was adamant, and I told him that I would handle the situation as best I could.

I saw each delegation as it arrived in Washington before the meeting and went over with it the plans for the conference. I told each group that I was asking the chairman of each delegation to serve on a committee on committees. I told them the State Department had worked out the organization, subject to approval or change by the Conference.

The chairman of the Soviet delegation, A. D. Krutikov, the forty-year-old Vice Commissar of Commerce of the USSR, was reluctant to serve as chairman of one of the working committees. His delegation, he said, would not take an active part in the conference but would listen to the program with interest. I told him I thought he ought to chair a committee, because Russia was one of the most important of the fighting allies. He said that Russia was about half overrun by Hitler's army at that time. The next day he agreed to serve and he did unusually good work as chairman of one of the main working committees.

The Conference met at Hot Springs on Tuesday, May 18, 1943. I addressed the first general session, urging that we consider both wartime and long range needs. I pointed out that by exchanging ideas the forty-four nations could be mutually helpful. I emphasized conserving and rebuilding the soil as the only way to assure an adequate diet for the hungry people of the world. Dr. Joao Carlos Muniz of Brazil responded beautifully, thanking this country and especially President Roosevelt for calling the Conference and expressing his hope for a permanent international food organization.

I had asked Mr. Kelschner of the State Department to be ready after the initial speeches to ask each of the visiting delegation to stand, so the delegates might see each other for the first time. He said that was not usually done at this kind of a meeting and he could not bring himself to do it. I took the list from him and one by one called off the names of the nations and asked its delegation to stand. When the name of Australia was called and the delegation stood, there was a great cheer, and the same was true of each delegation. Everyone seemed impressed. France was then completely overrun by the Germans; General DeGaulle and another general in exile had named the French delegation. The cheer following their introduction almost took the roof off. A spirit of enthusiasm and friendliness seemed to be generated by the exercise, and it gave us a good start. All the leading newspapers carried complete accounts of the proceedings; even Mr. Kelschner admitted afterwards that it went over well.

Even before the Conference began, some of the newsmen complained about the closed conference. They were not satisfied by the full briefing at the end of each working day. Publicity about the conference had not been good. After two days, I asked Dean Acheson to request Under Secretary Sumner Welles to ask the President to modify the ban. Welles refused, saying he had made that request twice before and he might get thrown out if he went back again. Mr. Acheson, as Assistant Secretary of State, did not want to authorize the change himself.

I telephoned Mr. Byrnes in Washington and told him about the unfavorable publicity and suggested throwing the session open. He said I was in charge and I should do what I thought was right. He advised against calling the President because it might embarrass him to make the change. I then announced the change to the press representatives. They seemed highly pleased, and after that the Conference got only favorable publicity.

Many of the delegates mingled in the large lobby both before and after dinner; we visited in the reception room after work; I requested different delegates to sit at my table at mealtime. We all acted like one big family.

The working committees made the place a beehive of activity. H. H. Bennett, Director of the Soil Conservation Service, addressed a general meeting. Many resolutions were considered and recommended, and the main body unanimously approved them. At the final session early in June, I addressed the Conference, thanking them for their cooperation and emphasizing our free discussions and our unanimous agreement as remarkable accomplishments. The details of the operation of the Food Conference have been published many times and need not be repeated here.

During the Conference I invited the entire Russian delegation to my apartment, along with Dean Acheson and Mike McDermott. Mr. Krutikov had a delightful sense of humor and I learned a few Russian words and phrases from him at our informal sessions. He invited me to fly back to Russia after the Conference or to come after the war. I asked whether they would really let me see Russia if I came. He replied that most visitors came looking for something to criticize, but that a visiting friend was different. He would go with me and let me see anything I asked to see. I said I might come, but after the war our officials and theirs developed such angry differences that I did not want to go.

The single most important action of the Conference was the adoption of a resolution calling for a charter for a permanent world food organization. The permanent organization was to be effective when twenty-nine of the forty-four nations ratified the charter, and any other nation might join later. I appointed the charter committee to begin work immediately. After several months the governments of more than twenty-nine nations approved the charter as drafted by the committee; in 1945 a permanent organization was formed and named The United Nations Food and Agriculture Organization (FAO).

By 1970 the permanent organization of the FAO had more than one hundred member nations. It has helped with marketing problems, especially the distribution of surplus commodities such as wheat and cotton, and it has been a clearinghouse for information about food production, accomplishing much.

The FAO sponsored a world wide program of feeding the hungry and called international conferences in 1958 and in 1963. Fourteen hundred delegates from 103 nations attended the 1963 conference in Washington. President John F. Kennedy and the President of India spoke at the morning session. I spoke in the afternoon and was presented a plaque as President of the Hot Springs Conference in 1943, where the movement began. That plaque is now on display at the Homestead Hotel in Hot Springs, Virginia.

Everyone was in high good humor as the Conference adjourned on June 3, 1943. We had just received an invitation to the six hundred delegates to attend a reception in their honor at the White House. Practically all the delegates attended. We all crowded into the assembly room at the White House, where the President made a speech thanking the delegates and complimenting them on the success of the Conference. We were then told that a further reception would be held in the back garden where the President would greet each of the delegates personally. I still wondered if the President would criticize me for opening up the Conference to the newsmen contrary to his specific instructions. I was asked to lead the delegates into the garden. As I reached the President he smiled, shook hands heartily and said, "Congratulations, Marvin, I think you did a grand job." The change of rules was not mentioned.

Chapter XXVII

WAR FOOD ADMINISTRATION

Soon after my return from Hot Springs, I was told by Mr. Byrnes that Chester Davis was unhappy in his work and was threatening to resign as War Food Administrator. I spent Sunday afternoon in his apartment at the Shoreham Hotel urging him to stay. The new mandatory ceilings on major farm commodities were making it difficult for him to function. He did not mind being placed under Mr. Vinson, but Vinson was so busy he had delegated most of the agricultural problems to assistants, one of whom in particular took delight in throwing his weight around. Another hateful problem was squabbles in the Department of Agriculture. On top of these troubles, Davis told me his health was not good, but he added that out of regard for me, he would continue to try.

He kept the post for a short time, but finally, after a late evening conference with Mr. Byrnes and others, at which it was thought most of his problems had been satisfactorily adjusted, Mr. Davis' letter of resignation to the President was delivered at the White House gate, effective in the fall. The President was irritated and he told Byrnes he had already signed a letter accepting Mr. Davis' resignation effective immediately.

The President called me to say he was appointing a new United States War Food Administrator, adding facetiously that the choice was between Herbert Hoover and me. I responded that Mr. Hoover had had a lot of experience. He laughed and said that I must take it. He suggested that I should resign, and that he would later reappoint me to the place I then held or a better one. I said the way he had the food job set up, no man could hold it for six months and then be confirmed to any other position. He laughed again and said, "You can."

I suggested Spike Evans. The President said he was not well enough known. He had a similar answer to the other names I suggested. I still hesitated. He said, "Go over there for one year and straighten it out, and then we'll talk about it." I said, "I'd like to be a member of the Mobilization Committee." He agreed. He also agreed to one or two other changes. In the circumstances I reluctantly accepted the assignment.

I asked Chester Davis to stay for a week or two and help me get started. He told me he would do anything in the world for me, but after the way the President treated him, he had no choice but to go back immediately to his position as President of the Federal Reserve Bank in St. Louis. The President had accepted his resignation effective immediately and he felt he had no authority to do anything else. I was sworn in early the next morning. Quite a group of officials had gathered in the conference room of the Department of Agriculture. I made a short talk to the group, asking their help and cooperation and expressing the hope for a united effort.

I began work immediately. The Executive Order had authorized the War Food Administrator to bring in any additional assistants he might need. I asked some of Chester Davis' special assistants to stay, but most of them were on leaves of absence at Davis' personal request and insisted on leaving.

Under the original Executive Order, the War Food Administrator was Chairman of the Allied Food Board, which allocated food to the armed forces, the civilian population and to our primary allies. Claude Wickard had generously permitted the transfer of additional duties to War Food. These included the storage of foods, transportation to ports and loading on ships, the purchase of all lend-lease and allied food, and the responsibility for any food that might still be on ships which had been torpedoed and came limping back into port with broken packages. Once these responsibilities were shifted to War Food, no agency was willing to take any of them back.

I began looking for the best transportation expert in the United States. Nearly everyone agreed it was Mr. Mark Upham, Eastern Manager of Proctor and Gamble. I immediately telephoned President Richard R. Depree of Proctor and Gamble in Cincinnati, and asked for Mr. Upham. He said Upham was one of his best men and he could not spare him. He had already permitted 150 of his men to go into government war service. I told him I had not wanted the job I had, that we all had a great deal at stake, and that I wanted Mr. Upham tomorrow morning. Mr. Depree replied that Upham was in Philadelphia and would be in my office at 9 o'clock the next day. The next morning, Mark Upham walked into my office on schedule. He did a magnificent job for a year and then Mr. Depree agreed to let him stay a few months longer.

Soon after beginning work as War Food Administrator, I decided we could eliminate duplication and overlapping by a thirty-minute daily conference of about twenty of the regular division heads. We met each morning at 9:30 to talk over problems. We would determine which of the Department heads would handle a particular matter without overlapping. After the first year, with things working smoothly, we found we could accomplish the same effect with three meetings, and later only one meeting, a week.

We were still having trouble with the 15 cent differential in the price of corn, which was not moving properly. Finally I suggested that we raise the price 10 cents a bushel and that we absorb the difference in freight from the great corn-producing areas to places in the east. We did not like subsidies; the farmers did not like them. But the President and Mr. Byrnes insisted that we use them in some instances from funds available in the Reconstruction Finance Corporation. After much discussion, we adopted the proposed plan; chickens, turkeys, and livestock in the East received the needed corn, and the plan operated without a hitch.

Congress had authorized the fixing of ceiling prices on basic farm commodities but it also fixed minimum prices below which certain perishable commodities, such as eggs, should not go. When named commodities reached the floor level, the War Food Administrator was instructed to buy them at floor price. One morning I learned the buyers had agreed among themselves to retire from the market and not to purchase any eggs unless they could get them at less than the fixed price.

My people were worried about what to do; they had been tendered that day 1400 carloads of eggs. I told them to buy the eggs. We would store all the eggs we could; then we would powder all we could dehydrate, and turn the rest into chicken feed and fertilizer. The commercial egg handlers and processors did not believe we would buy, and we had to show them. Before we had bought one hundred carloads, they came back into the market, and we had no further trouble.

We had another serious problem. With millions of young men going into the armed forces and the good wages paid in war industries, we had a great shortage of farm labor. We brought in 75,000 farm workers from Mexico, and several thousand from Cuba, Jamaica, and other places. We had to pay transportation, be responsible for them while they were in the United States, and return them home. The demand kept increasing. The Boy Scouts worked in the berry and fruit fields in the East; they did so well they were asked to return the following summer. Later on, a number of the factories asked for permission to employ foreign workers; after clearance with the immigration officials, this was done.

Each year, beginning in 1943, notwithstanding the shortage of labor, our people produced from 20 to 40 percent more food than ever before. The demand for food for war purposes was tremendous. Just after our armed forces had landed in Italy, I received a wire from General Dwight D. Eisenhower asking that I ship 30,000 barrels of flour to the forces in Italy. I had to wire all over the United States to get that much flour, but we got it on the move at the first call.

In December 1943, President Jeffers of the Union Pacific Railway Company, who had been called in several months before to solve the synthetic rubber problem, announced that synthetic rubber had been successfully produced from petroleum and that he was going back to his former position. The next day I was called to Mr. Byrnes' office to be confronted with a number of officials, including Bernard Baruch and Harry Hopkins. Byrnes announced that they were asking me to allot 50,000 tons of sugar and 160 million bushels of wheat for industrial alcohol to be used in making synthetic rubber. They all laughed when I told them of President Jeffers' statement that he had solved the synthetic rubber problem.

I was appalled at the magnitude of the task they were handing me. I had just finished alloting the civilian quota of sugar, which was already in short supply. They explained to me the plan to land in Europe and the need for rubber tires for 600,000 wheeled vehicles. I asked if I could explain to the public why so much wheat and sugar were suddenly being called for and they told me no, not one word. I said I did not know whether I could weather the storm, but I would do the best I could. They made one concession: I would be required to release these commodities only as they were being used, not all at once. As I walked away from that meeting, I think I was as blue as I had ever been in my life. But somehow it all worked out.

About this time I was very pleased to receive the following voluntary letter from Bernard Baruch, the advisor to Presidents:

October 12, 1944

My dear Judge Jones:

You certainly have done a good job as Food Administrator — with little noise — but with great effect.

I do not see you as much as I would like to, but there is nothing to talk to you about because you undertook a job, and you have done it. I congratulate you and want to say how deeply I appreciate your very fine efforts.

I wish our paths crossed oftener, but my feet only lead me where there is trouble I can help avoid. You don't need any help, because you see far ahead and act before the trouble occurs.

Again my congratulations to you.

Sincerely yours,
/s/ BERNARD M. BARUCH

I received a comparable letter from him on March 17, 1945. Among other things he said, "I wish everything would go as smoothly as you have been running your show."

We had a problem of sufficient food storage for perishable products, with constant danger of spoilage. Another problem was with broken and leaking packages. We were loading at one time more than twelve ships in New York Harbor. Rather than send broken packages back to warehouses, we hired Lynch, Donohoe and Dee, who employed 150 men on the docks in New York to repair defective packages so they could be immediately reloaded onto ships.

By early 1945 we had approximately twelve million men under arms. Since they were on the move, it took practically twice as much per man to furnish food for them; and they had first call on food supplies.

Another problem was to get balanced production. If we got too much production in one line we would have danger of spoilage. We had to persuade farmers to emphasize foods most needed for war services. We had to find support of the different divisions of the Department of Agriculture and of the thousands of county and community committees all over the country.

We were very proud of the results achieved; we felt grateful to farmers, including livestock and dairy people, who actually produced the food and made possible this wonderful record of production and distribution. Great credit also should go to the dedicated men and women in the War Food Administration.

At the end of the first year I went to see President Roosevelt. He was writing at his desk. I said, "Mr. President, my year as War Food Administrator is up." He looked up and said, "You know they are shooting boys in Europe who desert on the field of battle." Then he smiled and said, "You go back and finish the job. At least stay until the war in Europe is over."

As War Food Administrator, I became one of the few men who have served in an official capacity in all three branches of the Federal Government, the legislative, executive, and judicial. My friend Congressman Leo Allen of Illinois once asked me how many men had served in all three branches. I replied I had no idea. He then asked the Library of Congress. Its research division was able to find only six men in our history who had done so. It could not guarantee that was everyone, but that was all they were able to find.

Chapter XXVIII

JUDICIAL SERVICE

As indicated earlier, I was appointed by President Franklin D. Roosevelt to a judgeship on the United States Court of Claims on April 9, 1940, and the appointment was confirmed by the Senate on the following day. However, at the earnest request of President Roosevelt, I deferred qualifying and assuming the duties until January 1, 1941.

Upon the retirement of Chief Judge Whaley, I was appointed Chief Judge of the United States Court of Claims by President Harry S Truman and was sworn in on July 10, 1947. I served in that capacity until July 14, 1964, when I became Senior Judge of United States Courts, subject to assignment by the Chief Justice of the United States to serve on any United States Court of Appeals or United States District Court. President Lyndon Johnson appointed my successor as Chief Judge of the Court of Claims a longtime friend Wilson Cowen, who still serves in that capacity.

Perhaps it will be appropriate at this point to describe briefly the Court of Claims and its work. While it is a very important court, it was not well known for many years. The Court was established by Congress on February 24, 1855. Before that, our courts enforced the doctrine of sovereign immunity from suit, based upon the doctrine that "the King can do no wrong."

Between 1855 and 1865, the Court of Claims judgments were not final, and there was no appeal to the Supreme Court. During that ten-year period, it was generally treated as a legislative court, but in 1865 Abraham Lincoln recommended and secured the passage of a law making the United States Court of Claims a full constitutional court, with power to render final judgments and the right of direct appeal to the United States Supreme Court. Lincoln then added that the new law represented the conscience of the nation. In referring to the history of the Court of Claims a century later, Chief Justice Warren reiterated this thought: "The establishment of the Court of Claims 112 years ago represented the stirring of the conscience of a nation."

There are two divisions to the Court of Claims. First, the Court has fifteen trial commissioners, who are really trial judges, who are sent all over the United States and to foreign countries for the convenience of litigants. These judicial officers make findings of fact, recommend conclusions of law and under the statutes and rules of the Court write opinions. Second, the appellate division has seven judges. If neither party excepts to the findings and conclusions of the commissioner, and frequently they do not, the Court may adopt and issue his opinion as the opinion of the Court. However, either party has the right to have both his findings and conclusions reviewed by the judges of the Court.

The Court of Claims has jurisdiction over suits against the government for many millions of dollars, sometimes for as much as 100 millions. It covers practically all government contracts. For years it had exclusive jurisdiction over all suits for recovery of income taxes, but, because of the vast number of suits being filed, an amendment was adopted with our approval granting concurrent jurisdiction in refund cases to United States District Courts. Most of the larger claims are still filed in the United States Court of Claims. We have exclusive jurisdiction of appeals from the Indian Claims Commission, and we have jurisdiction over suits for retirement pay and many other types of cases, as provided by the statutes.

Senior Judge

When I retired as Chief Judge of the Court of Claims in 1964, I was in good health and did not want to get pulled in for vagrancy, so I decided I would continue to work. Under the law I could retire straight, sit in a rocking chair and do nothing, or I could by choice go on the Senior Judge List and be subject to assignment by the Chief Justice to serve on any U. S. court where additional help may be needed if I were willing to serve on that court at that particular time.

At the conclusion of the 1964 conference of Chief Judges of Circuit Courts throughout the country which meets annually in Washington, the Chief Justice announced that I was going on the Senior

Judge List and would be subject to assignment by him to sit on any U. S. court in the country where needed. The Chief Judges of five different circuit courts immediately requested that I accept assignment to the circuit with which they were connected.

The Chief Justice then said, "The Supreme Court of the United States has unanimously agreed to request Judge Jones as Senior Judge to hear the facts and write up a record in a suit between Louisiana and Mississippi." In a four-mile stretch beginning just below Natchez, Mississippi, one well had been drilled from the Louisiana bank nearly 2,500 feet in slant or directional drilling under the bed of the stream. Nearly a million dollars worth of oil had been extracted from the one well. The dispute was who was entitled to the oil.

There had been no survey of this area for a ten-year period. No further drilling would be made in the oil-rich area until the issue had been decided. There were several riparian owners on the Mississippi side who had rights to the middle of the river. The Chief Justice said it would be a difficult case, but he thought I would find it interesting. He thought the work would take a year or more. The Mississippi River winds like a serpent between Cairo, Illinois, and the Gulf, and these bends tend to grow larger. In order to simplify the matter the United States government had built several cut-offs between Cairo, Illinois, and the Gulf — in fact fifteen different cut-offs. The one just above the oil area was a four-mile cut-off that eliminated a nineteen-mile bend. The fifteen cut-offs reduced the length of the river between Cairo, Illinois, and the Gulf by about two hundred miles. The Supreme Court asked me to take the evidence, write a history of the legal questions involved, make findings of fact, and determine where the boundary was during each of the previous ten years when no survey of the river existed. The boundary had changed back and forth some 3,000 feet during the ten-year period. They also requested that I write recommended conclusions of law and an order to be entered by the Supreme Court.

This I did. The report was unanimously adopted by the Supreme Court of the United States. The report contains about sixty pages. It is being used as a pattern in one or two other cases that have been filed. All of this evidence and the findings took the greater part of the first year after I went on the Senior Judge List.

The briefs in the Supreme Court on the Master's Report were submitted in the Spring term of 1966, and the report was unanimously approved on April 18, 1966.

During the years since I became Senior Judge, I have sat at different times in more than two hundred cases in the United States Courts of Appeals in different sections of the country. This included thirty-three cases in Los Angeles and San Francisco at various times, more than thirty cases in two different years in Denver, eighteen in Oklahoma City, twenty-one in Fort Worth, and thirty-four cases in Richmond.

In the proceedings of the United States Courts of Appeals, the hearing of briefs and arguments are but a small part of the work involved. This is complex legal work in one of its highest refinements. We usually sat in panels of three and divided the cases among the members of the panel. In many instances there would be dissents or disagreements. In such cases it became necessary to exchange opinions and send copies of dissents and get copies of reports from each appellate judge in the circuit. Since the summer of 1971 I have worked less than normally, but I still do considerable work.

FINIS

ANNOTATION by J. M. Ray

Judge Jones wishes to publish another detailed volume later dealing with his court service. These memoirs would hardly be complete, however, without comment concerning his performance on the Court of Claims.

Chief Judge Wilson Cowen suggests that Judge Jones' two greatest contributions to the status and prestige of the Court of Claims were the law declaring it a Constitutional Court and the construction of the new building. Judge Jones was the principal mover in obtaining enactment of a statute in 1953 which relieved the Court of Claims from what he considered to be a mistaken holding made in the early 1880's that it was a legislative court, rationalized under Article I of the Constitution, and declaring it to be a Constitutional Court as authorized by Article III. The statute declared that it was in fact an Article III court as set out in an amendment following the Civil War giving the Supreme Court jurisdiction of appeals from the Court of Claims. On appeal the Supreme Court sustained the 1953 Act.

Chief Justice of the United States Earl Warren, speaking at the dedication of the courts building in 1967, after formally greeting Chief Judge Cowen, Judge Rich and others, said, "and last but not least, the father of this great building, Chief Judge Jones of the Court of Claims, retired. It is generally agreed that Senior Judge Jones was almost solely responsible for obtaining the appropriation for the beautiful new building for the Court of Claims and the Court of Customs and Patent Appeals on Madison Place across Lafayette Square only a few steps from the White House."

Chief Judge Cowen wrote about his predecessor, Judge Jones: "Judge Jones' opinions will rank with those of any judge of any court in clarity, readability, brevity with thoroughness, and general appeal. His opinions were enlivened with humorous anecdotes, references to the classics, earthy stories from his boyhood days, and philosophical reflections. Newspaper columnists seldom write about judicial opinions, but Judge Jones' opinions had so much reader appeal that they were often featured in a column in the *Washington Evening Star* written by a man who called himself 'The Rambler.'" [1]

In one case involving claims for back pay on the part of Korean War prisoner turncoats, he said: "The law has for its primary purpose the ends of justice; otherwise it is as useless as a child trying to grasp a handful of sunlight.... If it fails in this one thing it fails in everything." [2] We see the same point again in a case where a husband decided to accept a reduced pension so that his wife would have a living after his death, filled out the request in his own handwriting, and died before his request could be acted upon. The court ordered the pension for the widow, with Chief Judge Jones commenting, "The law is a vehicle for reaching the ends of justice." [3] It is Judge Jones' feeling that truth, equity and fair dealing are the hallmark of action in all three branches of our government.

Judge Jones would see that justice was done if he could arrange it at all. A woman worked two weeks for the Government before it was discovered she was a citizen of Austria and non-citizens were barred from employment by the 1952 Deficiency Appropriation Act. The Court held there was an implied contract, an obligation when goods or services are accepted and used for the benefit of the user. Speaking for the court, which had unanimously ordered payment, Judge Jones made the following comment: "Plaintiff worked 12 days. The defendant received the benefit of her services. She has not been paid. Since the pioneer's ax first rang in the wilderness of America the honoring of real obligations has been a tradition of her people." [4]

Judge Jones invariably sought true justice; he was impatient with tortuous legal logic. A Kentucky coal dealer's widow sued for the price of 100 tons of coal at $2 per ton. As usual the Government voucher was delayed several months. The coal dealer had sold the coal to the Government at cost. The coal dealer needed the money. The postmaster personally helped the dealer to borrow money at the bank with the understanding that the bank would be repaid when the voucher was received. The Acting Comptroller General refused to issue the voucher, contending that since the postmaster had helped the coal dealer borrow the money the Government obligation had thus been paid.

The Judge thought the Acting Comptroller General's letter was "singularly free from any suspicion of logic"; the coal dealer died and his widow sued. Said Judge Jones: "This method of settling government obligations is so novel that, if reduced to practice, it should be patentable. It would solve many national problems. The holder of a government obligation at one time or another is usually in need of money. He borrows money at the bank, and ergo, the Government's obligation is settled." [5] The widow got her money.

In another case, where the Army contended that its official representative had taken the disputed action in his personal and not in his official capacity, Chief Judge Jones commented wryly, "For the Army to contend and to provide by regulation that it is not liable since it did not act in its official capacity would be like a man charged with extra-marital activity pleading that whatever he may have done was done in his individual capacity and not in his capacity as a husband." [6]

On another occasion, Judge Jones observed, "Plaintiff takes a simple technical wording of a lease, carries it along the road to a pure legalism, and from there on to an absurdity. Somewhere along the way the spirit of the law is lost, falls into a dreamless sleep, and lies in an unmarked spot." [7]

Judge Jones throughout his years on the Court, as in his service in Congress, maintained a wholesome respect for American business enterprise. He felt, he said in one opinion, that the fabled maker of the better mousetrap would probably starve under modern conditions before the public learned he was in the woods, or be like the bashful boy who threw his sweetheart a kiss in the dark: he knew what he was doing but nobody else did.

In another case, Judge Jones delivered the Court's opinion in a suit to recover profits denied to the Lord Manufacturing Company by wartime price controls. Performances like that of the company here had helped to make our nation strong. Plaintiff's story was almost like a Horatio Alger novel. "Along with many other Americans we have unstinted admiration for the genius, the persistence, and the industry of a man of the type of H. C. Lord." [8]

A 1969 Circuit Court of Appeals case, participated in by Judge Jones by designation of the Chief Justice, dealt with Charles Lesley, an unlettered broomcorn cutter. In 1950 at the age of 19, he and an older boy were jointly charged in the state court with attempted robbery with firearms, but the other boy was tried separately. During seven days in jail, Lesley saw no lawyer and did not know he was entitled to one. He talked only to the sheriff, who told him if he stood trial he might get 99 years or even a death sentence, but, if he pleaded guilty, he, the sheriff, would persuade the county attorney to recommend a sentence of 40 years in prison. The badly frightened boy, who had never seen a court in session, agreed. He pleaded guilty and the judge sentenced him to 40 years in prison. He was immediately sent to the penitentiary.

Lesley served in prison 14 years when he was given a brief parole. A Texas lawyer told him his constitutional rights had been violated. Some time later a prominent Oklahoma City lawyer was assigned to represent him. He filed habeas corpus proceedings and asked for a complete discharge on the ground that the 1950 proceedings were illegal; the state courts, both trial and appellate, denied the writ. The attorney then filed suit in the United States District Court at Oklahoma City in 1968. He asked for the record but there was nothing except the minutes of the court. The District Judge then ordered a hearing in 1968. At the hearing the judge who had sentenced Lesley in 1950 said he remembered the case because the average sentence in similar cases in 1950 was four years. The judge said "the boy seemed confused and looked like someone had scared the daylights out of him." Yet the judge had sentenced him to 40 years in prison. The sheriff did not testify. The county attorney had died.

The case reached the United States Court of Appeals and was briefed and argued in the spring of 1968. The Court unanimously set aside the proceedings as illegal and ordered the prisoner discharged immediately, but withheld the effective date of the order 120 days to give the state authorities an opportunity to set aside their previous action and officially discharge Lesley if they saw fit. He was released in September 1968. In his concurring opinion in this case Judge Jones said: "When an inexperienced, frightened youth, without a criminal record, without counsel on a plea of guilty, without any evidence being taken is assessed a sentence of 40 years in the penitentiary in the revealing circumstances disclosed here, it is enough to stagger credulity. In the great novel, *Les Miserables*, Jean Valjean who had stolen a loaf of bread to feed his sister's children was arrested and sentenced to prison. Victor Hugo, the author, makes the following comment: 'There are in our civilization terrible hours. They are those mournful moments when society consummates its withdrawal from and pronounces shipwreck upon a human soul. Jean Valjean was given five years in the galleys.' That was fiction. Here we are dealing with facts, but the human equation runs through it all. In law, as in life, all facts and circumstances must be examined before just conclusions are reached. When the light of reason and the logic of analysis are brought to bear on the facts of record, they preclude any other reasonable conclusion that Lesley did not fully comprehend the need of an attorney and did not intelligently waive his right to court-appointed counsel, and finally a 40-year sentence in the circumstances borders on cruel and unusual punishment and certainly would deny the defendant due process and equal protection of the law." [9]

Perhaps the most significant and revealing opinion written by Chief Judge Jones was his dissent from the majority of the court in a case involving the League of Women Voters. The League sought exemption from income taxes on the ground that it was primarily an educational organization. The majority held it was not exempt; the nub of its decision was that the League was substantially involved in influencing legislation. Judge Jones did not question the conclusion, except to say the League did not work in its own interest. Human freedom was hard won; it must be maintained by "eternal vigilance"; and a cultivated mind is essential to the preservation of democracy. He commented: "The League of Women Voters is a completely unselfish organization operating almost exclusively in the public interest. It is clearly not the type of organization which the Congress meant to exclude from the benefits of the tax-exemption section. The activities of the League are in no sense partisan. It is almost wholly educational in its nature." [10] Such words reveal a deep understanding of the essence of the democratic process; how better to achieve such a perspective than by 24 years of responsive service in high elective office?

Judge Albert V. Bryan, a judge of the Fourth Circuit wrote Judge Jones on September 8 following his retirement: "The engaging charm you gave to the sessions of the Court of Claims will be emulated but never equalled. Nor can the gentleness and understanding — albeit its firmness — of your tolerance of the views of others opposing yours ever be matched. Such traits evince a character sterling and coveted. Good health and Godspeed in your retirement."

Federal District (later Circuit) Judge J. Braxton Craven, Jr., wrote him from North Carolina in April 1966: "I very much admire the style of your concurring opinion. I admire writing so much that I sometimes think I am a frustrated novelist. Most lalwyers and judges, including me, spend their lives in an effort for accuracy with the result that the English language suffers considerably. Most opinions sound like tedious Gothic. Judge Bryan is an exception to the rule, and so are you. Yours 'sings' a little, and is a welcome relief."

Judge James R. Durfee, a judge of the United States Court of Claims (Appellate Division), on October 23, 1968, wrote Senior Judge Jones the following letter on the occasion of the unveiling of his portrait: "The work of the artist who painted your portrait may fade away in long years to come, but your own work here will never fade. As long as this court continues, and its new courthouse stands, men will still remember you as the 'master builder' of them both. When I too retire, I trust that you will still be sitting with us as our senior Senior Judge, and as the 'pater familias' of all of us at the court who have come to cherish your wise guidance and enduring friendship."

This, then, is a brief survey of the judicial service of Marvin Jones, begun in 1941 and still continuing in the summer of 1972. He is in his fifty-fifth year of continuous service in all three branches of the government of the United States. One can only rejoice that men who have led a career in the Congress like that of Marvin Jones can qualify to serve three decades as a Federal judge.

REFERENCES

[1] Letter, March 24, 1972.

[2] *Otho G. Bell, et al.* v. *The United States,* 149 Ct. Cl. 248 (1960); Marvin Jones, *Should Uncle Sam Pay — When and Why?* p. 120.

[3] *Elsie C. Sonnabend* v. *The United States,* 146 Ct. Cl. 622 (1959); Jones, *ibid.,* p. 97.

[4] *Elizabeth Norcross* v. *The United States,* 142 Ct. Cl. 763 (1958); Jones, *ibid.,* p. 41.

[5] *Lucy W. Belcher* v. *The United States,* 94 Ct. Cl. 137 (1941); Jones, *ibid.,* p. 39.

[6] *Emil Borden* v. *The United States,* 126 Ct. Cl. 902 (1953); Jones, *ibid.,* p. 146.

[7] *Realty Associates, Inc.,* v. *The United States,* 134 Ct. Cl. 167 (1956); Jones, *ibid.,* p. 130.

[8] *Lord Manufacturing Company* v. *The United States,* 114 Ct. Cl. 199 (1949); Jones, *ibid.,* p. 31.

[9] *Charles Dean Lesley* v. *State of Oklahoma and Ray H. Page, Warden, Oklahoma State Penitentiary,* 407 F. 2d 543 (1969).

[10] *League of Women Voters* v. *The United States,* 148 Ct. Cl. 561 (1960); Jones, *ibid.,* p. 65.

APPENDIX I: CONCLUSION

The reminiscences of Marvin Jones are instructive to the student of government and public affairs in general. Here we have an ambitious young man of humble beginnings, a farm boy, intelligent and well-made, with a possibility of an athletic career, turning seriously toward the law, finishing academic work and moving through law school on money he himself earned or borrowed and later repaid. He soon recognized that he could hold his own with his peers; and, before his law course was completed, he was drafted to teach a course for an ailing professor. He moved to a frontier community and grew with it. His law practice gave promise of his future career.

After a very few years the young lawyer ran for Congress from a vast district, stretching over 400 miles from his old home in Cooke County, near Dallas, to Dalhart, in the Northwest corner of the Texas Panhandle. And he won in the first primary over the incumbent Congressman and others.

One of his first responsibilities in Congress in 1917 was to vote on the Declaration of the World War. Through a long novitiate he served as a junior minority party member of Congress, shoulder to shoulder with congressional stalwarts like John Garner and Sam Rayburn, hitting a good lick here and another there, constantly alert to improve the condition of the farmer, to whose cause he steadfastly adhered throughout his public life.

His faithful and competent service was crowned by his succeeding in 1931 to the Chairmanship of the Committee on Agriculture. His boyhood ambitions to serve and his years of congressional apprenticeship all came to focus in this career achievement. We can see in retrospect that agriculture was girding itself for its greatest era, the time of the realization of its fair share of the rewards of the American economic system, not only through the national leadership of President Franklin Roosevelt, but also in the restricted field of agriculture through the knowledge, resourcefulness, expertise, dedication and congressional leadership of Marvin Jones. It would appear that, as the nation's need for leadership fortuitously appeared in FDR, so comparably did agriculture come into its own with Marvin Jones.

What did the young Marvin Jones bring to Congress? One thing he brought was a remarkable oratorical and forensic talent. In the days when athletic heroes had not yet developed and college heroes were debaters, competition for the Sul Ross watch at the University of Texas at Austin was keen, and the second best speaker did not win it. As a fledgling lawyer, he showed the profession in the Golden Spread a top drawer legal style. He won his first race against the entire field, including the incumbent congressman, by speaking long and arduously across a sprawling district. In Congress he was drafted frequently to speak elsewhere in support of Democrats after his own Democratic primary chores were done. The public testimony to his speaking prowess given in Evansville, Indiana, in 1918, is ample proof. The admiring tribute of Congressman Hatton Sumners after the stunning victory over the telegraph blitz by the organized meatpackers is perhaps the most convincing of all. No stumblebum could earn such praise.

Perhaps the most convincing testimony of all was Solicitor-General Stanley Reed's invitation to him to argue the AAA case before the Supreme Court. It is rare indeed that a congressman is considered for so complex and important a forensic assignment. After the Farm Bureau Federation's onslaught in the fight over the Soil Conservation Act of 1938, his plaint, delivered to the House on what amounted to an appeal on personal privilege, the "rising demonstration of approval" was ultimate witness to effective rhetoric. Here, as Marcus Cato phrased it, was a good man speaking well. Even to the very end of his congressional service, he was in demand, witness his enrollment in the barnstorming campaign with Henry Wallace in the fall of 1940.

Resourcefulness and courage are two of the prime requisites in the makeup of the successful congressman, and Marvin Jones was endowed with both. As a young man, coming into his life style, he took the practical approach to problems confronting him. He entered college from the "back door" because that was the side of the school he was on; but he was not long in becoming properly oriented. He sold stereopticons in summer to earn school money and learned how to influence people. Perhaps one of the most effective of the congressmen the nation has developed, John Garner, told the new President in early 1933 that Jones was one of the ablest congressmen and a great floor leader. And after his courageous display of virtuosity in the last lame duck session, FDR commented, "You must be a magician." And when they were seeking urgently for a "ball carrier" for the Sugar Act, all signs pointed to Marvin Jones, even though the bill was properly within the sphere of the Committee on Ways and Means, and not Agriculture.

When the Farm Bureau Federation, under the leadership of Ed O'-Neal, chose by main force to substitute its bill for the Committee's choice in 1938, not only did the Speaker, in answer to Secretary Wallace's appeal, defer to Committee Chairman Jones, but he also said, "The House has complete confidence in him." It was this way throughout his congressional career.

This wide acceptance of his leadership and confidence in his integrity was clearly in evidence in his first race for Congress; how else would his vast district have chosen a hitherto unknown young lawyer over all opponents? Republican Leader James Mann was early drawn to the earnest and able young Democrat, and befriended him in vital and subtle ways. Other opposition leaders also respected his integrity and high purpose. Bert Snell deferred to his importunings in helping to get a share of the tariff income for the farmer, and John Taber responded to his urgings in approving the $196 million deficiency appropriation after the invalidation of the AAA. "That's a lot of money," said Taber. And Jones responded, "Yes, but there are a lot of farmers and this is a big country." Accommodations of this sort are not made across party lines except in an atmosphere of mutual respect and friendship.

Much more predictable, and quite commonplace for Marvin Jones, was James P. Buchanan's backing of his power play in holding up Soil Conservation appropriations until Dr. Bennett agreed to a Dust Bowl regional administrative office in the Texas Panhandle. Any who might discount this ploy as a plum for the district overlook the uniqueness and urgency of soil conservation needs in the Dust Bowl.

Further illustrative of Jones' legislative prowess is his selection to manage the Sugar Act through the House. It was not his responsibility. It soon became obvious that it was FDR who chose him for the task because "you have a habit of getting quick action." The most significant aspect of the entire arrangement was State's and Agriculture's sending poorly informed and inexperienced men to the House hearing, assuming, that, now they had Marvin Jones in charge, the battle was already won. He, on the other hand, could only take one step at a time, and each step had to lead constructively forward.

The widespread cooperation shown to Marvin Jones on all sides was not tribute of vassals to a lord. It was the acquiescence of peers in the proposals of a resourceful and forthright parliamentary expert who always put the public's interest first. He concluded as a lad that farmers needed a special credit system. He refused in his first campaign to provide expensive mementos to voters. His espousal of the cause of the impecunious tenant farmer is most eloquent evidence of his devotion to principle, even in the face of carping critics who usually see the lowly as deserving of their meager lot. His unwillingness to stand by while processors reaped a windfall with the invalidation of the AAA is another case in point. The groundswell for the Frazier-Lemke bill was another: it just was not right, and Marvin Jones was one of the architects of its defeat.

The ultimate in Marvin Jones' legislative leadership was the Soil Conservation Act of 1938. It was not by accident that the invitation came to him to address the class at Harvard's Littauer School. His performance in passing this act was recognized as superb. He was challenged in his exercise of the public power rightfully his in the House Agriculture Chairmanship by the leadership of the potent Farm Bureau Federation. They tried in numerous ways to circumvent him. They pressured their captive Secretary, Henry Wallace, to appeal to the Speaker over Jones' head, without avail. They prevailed over the Senate in short order but in the House "they had picked the wrong man." Marvin Jones won that battle handsomely, as he did others, not by chicanery or summary dealings, but by being so true in his judgments and so right and fair in his dealings that even the capricious "Cotton Ed" Smith and later the kingpin of agricultural group pressure, Ed O'Neal, concurred in the course he had taken.

Marvin Jones' ability to handle people was much of his stock in trade. His teasing and then soothing touch with Secretary Wallace in toning down alarm over Senator Smith's threatened resolution requiring farm experience for administrators exemplifies one facet. Others are revealed in his masterful handling of "Cotton Ed" Smith; his restoring of order in the price-fixing effort for live cattle in the Washington meeting; his "Thanks, Marvin. You did a grand job" from the President after the historic Food Conference; and his thirty minute daily staff meetings in War Food to eliminate overlapping and duplication of effort.

There were many additional facets to Marvin Jones' complex relationships in government. He was indomitable: how else can one gauge his accomplishments in sending the Marine Band to Amarillo after the Huey Long filibuster sealed the doom of the deficiency appropriation bill to pay for the trip? A lesser man would not even have tried; even if he had, he would have got nowhere. He rarely hesitated to join battle against great odds. In the 1920's with his party in an almost hopeless minority he struggled, and sometimes won. In the Lame Duck session before Roosevelt's inauguration, he won the uphill battle in the House, with Speaker Garner urging him to postpone the effort. As War Food Administrator, he moved with alacrity to buy eggs and bluff down processors who were trying to destroy the floor price. And he knowingly and alone reversed the President's strictures against open publicity at the wartime International Food Conference.

The infinitely complex sequences of developments in governmental affairs shape the performances of individuals engaged in the process. The two major consequences that flowed from the invalidation of the AAA were, first, the windfall of profits to the processors and the effort to stop them, and, second, the necessity to obtain $196 millions to provide subsidies to farmers cooperating under the invalidated Act. The task of winnowing the way through the labyrinthine byways dictated by such circumstances falls to men who know the ropes, and none knew them as well nor wended his way through them as skillfully and unerringly as Marvin Jones.

One technique Marvin Jones mastered might be termed "dealing from strength." Once the opposition is on the run, win the contest decisively and conclusively. His method was presaged in the contest with the Bovina Justice of the Peace on behalf of the Turkey Track Ranch: when the J.P. was caught dead to rights in *ultra vires* action, beat him down to size with the biggest stick available, the threat to sue his bondsmen. Later, in Congress, the gentle suggestion to Senator John H. Bankhead that the Bankhead Cotton Control Act was possibly controversial cleared the way for the first big step toward realizing Jones' long-held dream of the farmer's fair share of the tariff; and then, with his fine instinct for the jugular, he nailed it down not with a vague authorization but by the words, "there is hereby appropriated annually."

Two other cases illustrate the use of the heavy weapon to win a point conclusively. One is the holding up of the annual appropriation for Soil Conservation to blast loose the adamant attitude of administrators of carving out administrative regions by state boundaries without regard to special problems of wind erosion. A second illustration of the power approach was precipitated by the Interior Department administrator who would not listen to proposals for small dams to be built from the $4 billion 880 million lump sum work relief bill. The pooling of strength with Congressman Joe Starnes to amend the bill to get special shares of the appropriation earmarked for favored projects was a rough but effective way to secure the promise from the President of later allocations. Sometimes, in the tumultuous confrontations of politics, the opposition will take notice only of the muzzle of a cocked blunderbuss.

Marvin Jones made many unique contributions to the cause of agriculture. Not the least of these was choosing his field of specialization early and sticking with it, becoming chairman of his committee when its time in history came, and bringing to this cause the myriad talents and resources which his performance so fully displayed. The list of the bills he pushed through to enactment speaks for itself; the marks of his contributions are all over each of them.

But in addition to his general unending service to agriculture, there are specifics that would never have seen daylight without Marvin Jones. Farm credit had been a lifelong goal; the ploy that made it possible was the battle during the first 100 days of the New Deal, joined by Marvin Jones against the Speaker's protest, to have the bill referred to Agriculture rather than to Banking and Currency. A chairman of Agriculture less determined on the point, not so fully persuaded of the necessity to break away from the traditional concepts of banking as usual, and one more inclined to comfort and shunning the arduous chore would have backed away from the contest, and the course of the history of agriculture in this country would have been greatly different.

Another program to which the personality of Marvin Jones was quintessential was the Small Lakes program, bludgeoned out of the huge $4 billion 880 million work relief pork barrel. It would never have appeared without him. Indeed, even after the pledge of allocation of funds by FDR it might well have been treated as a stepchild if he had not got it located in the Department of Agriculture until Secretary Ickes of Interior later saw the light and promised to straighten up and fly right.

The Bankhead-Jones Act, providing means for tenant farmers to buy their homes, had its roots in Valley View, where Marvin Jones was born and raised. Without him it would not have been conceived, nor would it have weathered the scorn of the well-to-do and been enacted into law. His affection for this program provided one of the reasons for his staying in Congress until late November 1940, to assure an adequate appropriation for another year. This espousal of the cause of the lowly and the powerless restores one's sometimes flagging confidence in democracy.

No lesser person than Marvin Jones could have withstood the successive immoderate attacks of the supporters of the Frazier-Lemke bill in 1936 and the Farm Bureau Federation's effort at domination of the government's agriculture program in 1938. Agriculture had long been served at the second table; their successes under the New Deal were heady tonic, and the temptation toward excessive demands was strong. Only a true and infinitely resourceful friend of the farmer could have held the line.

Still another totally unique contribution of Marvin Jones to our government was as War Food Administrator. No man of his time was as knowledgeable and as universally known, respected, accepted, and as talented for this work as he. He came to it belatedly and reluctantly, but he handled it with the full competence he had shown in all his other enterprises.

And finally Judge Jones made indelible marks on the Court of Claims. In addition to his wise and substantial contribution to the law proclaimed by the Court, under his leadership the Court emerged from its century of shadow as a legislative court to become legally a part of the constitutional court system. He approached with his customary thoroughness statutory reforms in the Court's procedure and jurisdiction. And, finally, he led in the successful effort to provide the handsome new

Court of Claims Building, dedicated in 1967.

The termination of Marvin Jones' congressional service represented in a sense a completed circle. He replaced as a youngster a congressman who had become Washington-oriented. In his own turn, such demands were being made on his time in Congress that he found difficulty in keeping his home district fences fully mended. He collected on the President's promise of "the job I wanted," and he was fortunate to be able to perform his administrative service during the war on leave of absence from it. His retirement from the Chief Judgeship came after long and arduous service, in his eightieth year. And his service in all three branches of the government earned the solemn verdict, "You did a grand job, Marvin."

APPENDIX II: VIGNETTES

Many vignettes have been shaped by Marvin Jones' words in these *Memoirs,* some of Jones himself and others of the many famous and interesting people he encountered in his long career.

The boy Marvin at his father's knee, learning that the American banking system was geared for businessmen, not for farmers.

The stripling Marvin, already with his eye on far places, on crossing a field where his brothers and sisters are chopping cotton, and being queried, "Where are you going?" and responding pertly, "I am going to Congress."

The powerful and gifted young college athlete, a doubtful starter because of injuries, winning Southwestern University's baseball game against the University of Arkansas in Fayetteville with a grandslam homerun.

Old Bill Davis of Gainesville seriously offering as a congratulatory telegram from a public home community gathering to his long-haired arch enemy, Joe Bailey, far away in Congress, "Dear Joe: Cut your hair and come home."

Senator Joe Bailey proclaiming wryly his inability to become a Christian because, "I would have to forgive old Bill Davis and I couldn't do that."

"Uncle Joe" Cannon, former Speaker of the House, serving out another decade, relaxed, respected and good-natured, at 87, squiring a centenarian former congressman down to the well of the House for recognition.

Champ Clark, a disappointed presidential aspirant, steeped in the minutiae of political history, convinced that the election of strong Sam Houston instead of temporizing James Buchanan to the presidency in 1856 would have markedly changed the course of American history.

Congresswoman Jeannette Rankin of Montana, in an almost inaudible voice, trying in violation of the House rules to explain her vote against the War Resolution in April 1917.

Level-headed Sam Rayburn supporting the World War I draft after boasting he would not do so if 90 percent of his voters favored it, and playfully explaining: ". . . but 95 percent of my people favor it."

The heckler's pert quip in response to Socialist Victor Berger's rhetorical question as to what the United States had got out of the World War, "Prohibition and the flu."

President Woodrow Wilson in company with three congressmen, taking a pad on his knee to write out a statement on Woman Suffrage.

Georges Clemenceau, Premier of France and former girls' college teacher in New England, 75, plump, wearing black gloves at his desk, and speaking beautiful English, bursting into riotous laughter at the Utah congressman's admission that he was not a Mormon, but a "Gentile with Mormon inclinations."

Republican Floor Leader James R. Mann in 1918, with tongue secretly in cheek, giving the earnest young Democrat Marvin Jones a hard time over the time zone law, just to make him look good to his voters back home.

John Garner, wise in politics, advising the neophyte congressman to stay out of the *Congressional Record* until the people's confidence in him had grown.

Hatton Sumners, looking less like a congressman than any, on being asked if Jones' new hat made him look like a statesman, responding, "No, I wouldn't say that. It goes as far as a hat can."

A new Republican congressman produced from Oklahoma by the 1920 Republican landslide, Manuel Herrick, after consuming a handful of sandwiches and a fruit decoration apple at the British Embassy addressing a liveried attendant with supreme gaucherie, "You shore did give us a fine feed."

On complimenting blind Oklahoma Senator Thomas P. Gore on a surpassing flight of eloquence, Marvin Jones, no mean speaker himself, being bowled over by the response, "Praise from Cicero himself is praise indeed."

Will Rogers in 1921 twitting President Harding on his golf and yachting with, "The next time I vote for a President, I'm going to vote for a seasick man with a wooden leg."

Minority Floor Leader Finis Garrett commenting on President Calvin Coolidge's State of the Union address to a Joint Session of Congress, "Longitude, latitude, platitude."

President Calvin Coolidge's calling in Marvin Jones and two other congressmen about an agricultural problem and showing surprising knowledge of the provisions of their proposed substitute bill and, despite his reputation for taciturnity, doing most of the talking for 30 or 40 minutes.

The staunch and determined maturing young Congressman resisting John Garner's importunate demand that he leave the Committee on Agriculture for another assignment, thus holding himself firmly in line for the future that awaited him as agriculture's all-time greatest protagonist.

William Gibbs McAdoo, son-in-law of Woodrow Wilson and able and ambitious politician, carrying a lasting grudge against Al Smith for wrecking his presidential hopes in 1924 and lining up California delegates in 1932 for old and warm friend John Garner and possibly in reserve for himself, if lightning should strike.

John Garner, causing consternation at the Chicago Democratic Convention by retiring early in Washington, asking not to be disturbed, and finally, after Dutch uncle talk with Sam Rayburn, saying he did not want to make any trade but, if they wanted to nominate him for Vice President, he would accept it.

Marvin Jones' first visit with Franklin Roosevelt at Hyde Park; his conclusion that Roosevelt was somewhat breezy, but soon realizing he had great substance.

Agriculture Dean William I. Myers of Cornell, FDR's original brains trust for agriculture, but summoned back shortly to the ivy-covered halls, "a truly great administrator."

Franklin Roosevelt, in the tremendous rush of the first "one hundred days," taking a copy of the newly completed draft of the Agricultural Adjustment Bill from his desk and quizzing the bill's authors about intended meaning of clauses, showing that he had not only read but had studied it.

Senator Huey Long, with "a quick, agile mind and a good memory," announcing on the Senate floor the names of five Louisiana congressmen who had, presumably in secret, agreed to oppose him, and stating flatly that none of the five would be members of the next Congress — and none were.

"Cotton Ed" Smith's threat of a Senate Resolution requiring five years of farm experience for Agriculture Department administrators; Henry Wallace's consternation arising therefrom, and Marvin Jones' teasing him and then reassuring him and later kidding old "Cotton Ed" about it.

Secretary Harold L. Ickes, the Old Curmudgeon, accepting in good grace the powerful Congressman Marvin Jones' evisceration of his grand plans for a Department of Conservation, refusing to counter with argument, and later cordially inviting him out to dinner.

Dewey Short's scornfully boasting of having crawled farther under the barn looking for eggs than John Rankin had traveled away from home.

John Rankin's confessing to having said to Mrs. Roosevelt that she had done the country more harm than any woman had ever done any country except Cleopatra, and if she had been as good looking she would have ruined the Republic, and then wondering innocently whether Mrs. Roosevelt may have disliked what he had said.

Henry Morgenthau's irascible protest at Marvin Jones' arrangement for a share of tariff proceeds to be earmarked for agriculture, and his continuing effort to undo it.

Marvin Jones' exceeding reluctance to undertake the arduous chore of floor leadership for the Sugar Act, melting away on FDR's request, "as a special favor to me." And Jones', "Of course I had to do it."

The Harvard professors and graduate students hanging on the words of the most effective Congressman of his time in an effort to learn how he had been able to defy and vanquish the powerful and rampant Farm Bureau Federation and its captive Agriculture Secretary Henry Wallace, and to take firmly under his wing the capricious and flamboyant "Cotton Ed" Smith.

A terribly harassed President Roosevelt, in the midst of World War II, petulantly accepting Chester Davis' resignation as War Food Administrator and urging Judge Marvin Jones to take over.

James F. Byrnes, former Supreme Court Justice, handling War Stabilization from the east wing of the White House, working long hours, with his alert mind and his talent for quick decisions, "the vital spark in the operative end of the war effort."

Bernard Baruch, hoary and prestigious elder statesman, covering the entire front of war administration, encouraging in adversity, helping when needed, and periodically congratulating warmly those like Marvin Jones who could hoe their own row.

The Chief Judge of the Court of Claims, already long in years of service, on retiring to the Senior Judge List in 1964, being besieged for commitments to serve by Chief Judges of Circuit Courts, who are requested in open meeting by the Chief Justice of the United States to stand back and await their turn until Judge Jones performs as Supreme Court Master the arduous, months-long task of adjudicating for the high court the oil-rights boundary dispute between Mississippi and Louisiana.

Judge Jones being presented at the Dedication of the Courts Building ceremonies in 1967 by Chief Justice of the United States Earl Warren as "the father of this great building, Chief Judge Jones of the Court of Claims, retired."

In 1972 Senior Judge Marvin Jones, the octogenarian whose mother lived to 102, moving somewhat more slowly on his appointed judicial rounds, an extraordinary public servant both in quality and durability, secure in the high regard of all who know him.

INDEX

Abilene, Ks., 15
Abolishing an agency of government, 50
Acheson, Dean, 154, 155
Agricultural Adjustment and Soil Conservation Act, 98
Agricultural Adjustment Act invalidated, 118
Agriculture, Com. on, 93, 132, 134, 146
Agriculture, Com. on, Chairman of, 173
Agriculture Credit Corp., 105
Agriculture, Dept. of, 110, 132, 133, 134, 147
Ahrens, A. H., 89
Alamo Society, debating, 10
Albert, King, of Belgium, 40
Allied Food Board, 147, 158
All-Inclusive New Farm Bill, 134
Alsace-Lorraine, 41
Amarillo, Tx., 15, 18, 20, 24, 41, 101, 102, 125, 134, 135
Amarillo, Tx., practiced law in, 13, 14, 15, 16
Amarillo Chamber of Commerce, 101, 125
American Bar Association, 48
American Farm Bureau Federation, 134
Anti-Saloon League, 37
Arkansas, University of, 11, 180
Armistice, the, November 11, 1918, 44
Armour and Co., 89
Armour, Phil, 65
Aswell, Dr., of La., 40
Atkeson, Rep. William O., 52
Bailey, Joseph W., 6, 14, 22, 23, 27, 180
Bailey, Mollie, circus owner, 27
Baker, Newton D., 83
Baltimore Convention, 1912, 54
Bank failures, 90
Bankhead Cotton Control Act, 177
Bankhead, Sen. John H., 112, 128, 142, 177
Bankhead-Jones Act, the, 129
Bankhead, Rep. William B., 49, 115, 117, 134, 142
Banking and Currency Com., 93, 94
Barkley, Alben W., 7, 38, 40, 74
Barrett, Leonidas C., law partner, 14
Baruch, Bernard M., 149, 151, 160, 183
Baruch, Bernard M., congratulations from, 161
Baseball, at Southwestern U., 11
Baseball, at Valley View, 2, 4
Baylor University, 11, 25
Bell, J. Ross, 1928 opponent, 79
Bell, Tom, twin of J. Ross, 79
Bennett, Dr. H. H., 106, 108, 109, 155
Berger, Victor, 37, 180
Billy the Kid, 15
Black, Rep. Eugene, 49

Bledsoe, State Sen. W. H., 57
Blue discharge for minors, 55
Board of Legal Examiners, 17
Bolshevism, 59
Bonus marchers, 87
Bootlegger, defense of a, 20
Bovina Justice of the Peace, 19, 177
Bravo Ranch, special master for, 14
Breaks of the Canadian River, 20
British Embassy, 53
Brooks Prize commencement debate, 10
Brooks, Dr. S. P., 25
Browning, Judge J. N., 14
Bryan, Judge Albert V., 171
Bryan, William Jennings, 54
Buchanan, Pres. James, 46
Buchanan, Rep. James P., 49, 108, 125, 175
Bureau of Mines, 58
Byrd, Sen. Harry, 110
Byrnes, James F., 147, 148, 149, 150, 151, 152, 154, 157, 183
Byrns, Speaker Joseph, death of, 117
Cairo, Il., 165
Campaign, 1920, 52
Campaign, 1928, 79
Campaign, 1932, 83
Campaign expenses, 1916, 30
Candidate for Floor Leader, Marvin Jones, 115, 118
Canadian, Tx., 17
Canadian River, breaks of the, 20
Cannon, "Uncle Joe," former Speaker, 47, 180
Canyon, Tx., 96
Cardoza, Justice, 119
Carew, Rep. John F., 84
Carlsbad Caverns, 140
Carr, Mary, Elm Grove teacher, 4
Carter, Rep. Charles D., 49
Case, Sen. Francis, 128
Ceiling price on farm products, 146
Ceiling price on live cattle, 148, 149
Chaplin, Charlie, 36
Chaumont, Pershing's hqs. at, 40
Chavez, Sen. Dennis, 101
Chesapeake and Ohio Railway, 124
China, 54
Circus the G. O. P., 71, 72, 73, 74
Clark, Speaker Champ, 32, 36, 45, 52, 54
Clark, Champ, on history, 46, 54
Clark, Champ, on Sam Houston, 46
Clark, Champ, on youth in Congress, 29, 32
Claremore, Ok., 64
Clay, Gen. Lucius, 149
Clemenceau, Georges, 40, 41, 180
Cobb, J. D., U. of Tx. debater, 12
Cockran, Rep. W. Bourke, 47
Cohen, Ben, 149

Cole, Cornelius, centenarian, 47
Commencement debate, Southwestern U., 10
Committees of farmers, 92
Committee on Agriculture, 106, 132, 134, 146
Committee on Banking and Currency, 146
Committee on Indian Affairs, 26
Committee on Interstate and Foreign Commerce, 140
Conchas Dam, 101
Confederate Veterans, 124
Conference Committee, 136, 138
Congratulations, Marvin, 156
Congress Hall Hotel, 46
Congress in wartime, 1917, 35
Congress, Race for, 22
Congressional Record, 48, 51, 111
Connally, Sen. Thomas, 85
Constitutional court, 167
Cooke County, Tx., 6, 26
Coolidge, Pres. Calvin, 52, 58, 74, 75, 76, 77, 78, 181
Coolidge, Mrs. Grace, 75
Cooper, Rep. Henry Allen, 34
Copley-Plaza Hotel, Boston, 105
Coronado celebration, 139
Costigan, Sen. Edward P., 133
Cotton research, 76
Court of Appeals, in Amarillo, 16
Court of Claims, 142, 146, 147, 163, 178
Cowen, Chief Judge Wilson, 109, 163, 167
Cox, James M., 52
Craven, Judge J. Braxton, Jr., 171
Crawford, J. E., 1905 debate partner, 10
Credits, system of farm, 67
Creel, George, 36
Crop Loan Act, 95
Cudahay, 65
Cummings, Rep. Fred, 132
Cummings, Atty. Gen. Homer, 118
Customs and Patent Appeals, Court of, 167
Dalhart, Tx., 26, 106, 108
Daniels, Amb. Josephus, 143
Daugherty, Harry, 71, 73, 80
Davis, Chester, 110, 118, 151, 157, 158, 183
Davis, John W., 70
Davis, William O., 23, 24, 180
Dawson Springs, Ky., 41
Daylight Saving Act, 43
Decatur, Tx., 27
Declaration of War, 33
Deferred service bonus, 87
Deficiency appropriation bill, AAA invalidation, 120, 121
Democratic National Congressional Committee, 42, 45
Democratic State Convention, 1920, 57

Dempsey, Jack, 107
Denver, Co., 166
Department of Agriculture, 132, 133, 134, 147
Department of Conservation and Public Works, 106
Department of State, 133, 153
Depree, Richard R., 158
Depression, the Great, 79, 90
Dewey, Thomas B., 7
Dodge City, Ks., 15
Draft, the, 1917, 36
Dressler, Marie, 36
Dumont, Tx., 29
Dundee, Tx., 25
Durfee, Judge James R., 171
Dust Bowl, 104, 106, 107, 108, 175
Early days, stories about, 17
Economic stabilization, 146
Edinburgh, Scotland, 41
Eggs, floor price on, 160
Eighteenth amendment, 37
Eisenhower, Gen. Dwight D., 160
Eiser Canal, 40
Election, 1936, 124
Ellerd, Reuben M., 1916 opponent, 24, 25, 26, 28, 29
Elm Grove, Tx., 4
El Paso, Tx., 43, 80, 82
Era, Tx., 4
Esch Act, 1919, 61
Evans, Silliman, 57, 85
Evans, Spike, 157
Evansville *Courier*, 42
Evansville, In., 42
Fahey, Charles, 149
Fairbanks, Douglas, 36
Fall, Albert B., 71, 106
Farley, James A., 84, 125
Farm Bureau Federation, 174, 183
Farm commodities, new markets for, 66
Farm credit, 6, 67, 115, 177
Farm Credit Administration Act, 95, 98, 142
Farm Credit Administration, executive order, 90
Farm credit reference battle, 93
Farm mortgages foreclosed, 90
Farm tenants, home ownership by, 128
Farwell, Tx., 18
Federal Land Banks, 93, 95, 99, 100
Federal Reserve Board, 99, 100, 116
Ferris, Rep. Scott, 63
First hundred days, New Deal, 98
First National Bank, Valley View, 5
Five-year plan, Cotton Ed Smith's, 103
Flood, Henry D. (Hal), 38
Food and Agriculture Organization, UN, 155, 156
Food Conference, First International, 152
Ford, Henry, 62, 66
Ford, Model T, 1916 campaign, 24, 26
Fordney-McCumber Tariff Act, 69

Fort Worth, Tx., 166
Frazier-Lemke bill, 115, 116, 175, 178
Freight cars, allocation of, 61
Freight rate discrimination, 31, 60, 140
Froelich, Dr., Littauer School, 138, 139
Fuller, Claude, 115
Fullingim, John, 101
Gainesville, Tx., 6, 23
Garner, John N., 33, 37, 48, 81, 83, 84, 85, 89, 124, 173, 181, 182
Garrett, Rep. Finis, 34, 76, 181
Gaston, Sarah, great-grandmother, 7
Gaston, William, auth. NC State song, 7
Gastonia, NC, 7
Georgetown, Tx., 9
German U-Boats, 31
Germany, declaration of war on, 33
Glass, Carter, 83
Glidden, Joseph, 15
Gold watch, ex-Gov. Ross, 93
Gore, Sen. Thomas P., 63, 64, 181
Goree, Tx., 27
Grand Canyon, 140
Grand Fleet, 41
Great Plains Committee, the President's, 109
Guleke, J. O., 109
Hamilton, Alexander, 114
Happy Warrior Nominating Speech, 70
Harding, Pres. Warren G., 52, 68, 69, 70, 181
Hardy, Rev., Ellerd supporter, 28
Harrison, Pat, 49
Harvard University, 138, 139
Hatch, Sen. Carl, 101
Hawkins, Docia, 7
Hays, Will, 73
Helium, 58
Herrick, Rep. Manuel, 53, 181
Highway 66, 64
Hill, John E., 109
Hinton, Carl, 101
Home Owners Loan Corp., 100
Home ownership by tenant farmers, 128
Homestead Hotel, Hot Springs, Va., 156
Hoover Bull Market, the great, 80
Hoover, Pres. Herbert C., 37, 79, 81, 157
Hoover, H. E., 17
Hopkins, Harry, 151, 160
Hot Springs, Va., 152, 153, 156
Houston, Sam, Champ Clark comments on, 46
Howard, Rep. William Schley, 35
Hub (Herbert) Jones, brother, 22
Hudspeth, Rep. Claude, 80
Hughes, Charles Evans, 31, 73
Hukriede, Rep. T. W., 52
Hull, Sec. Cordell, 131, 132, 152
Humphreys, Rep. Ben, 49
Hutchinson County, Tx., 18, 19

Hyde, Arthur M., Sec. of Agriculture, 81
Hyer, Dr. R. S., 9
Ickes, Sec. Harold L., 59, 106, 107, 128, 182
Inauguration, March 4, 1933, 91
Indian Affairs, Committee on, 26
Indian Claims Commission, 164
Indian Territory, Ok., 21
Intermediate Credit Discount Banks, 95
International Food Conference, First, 152
Interstate Commerce Commission, 31, 43, 60, 61, 62, 140, 141
Irrigation and Reclamation Division, 127
Italy, King of, 40
Jackson, Gen. Andrew, 55
Jackson, J. R., 32
James, Sen. Ollie M., 34
Jeffers, Pres. of Union Pacific, 160
Johnson, Pres. Lyndon, 163
Johnson, Wendell, classmate, 26
Jones-Costigan Sugar Act, 131
Jones, Delbert, brother, 10, 12
Jones, Docia, mother, 1, 2, 7, 8
Jones, Frank Pierce, brother, 1
Jones, Herbert (Hub) King, brother, 1
Jones, Horace K., father, 1, 5, 6, 7
Jones, J. T., cousin, 102
Jones, James Edmonston, great-grandfather, 5
Jones, Metze (Neely), sister, 1
Judicial service, 163
Jutland, Battle of, 41
Kahn, Julius, 36
Keith's Vaudeville Theatre, 68
Kelschner, State Dept. official, 154
Kendrick, Sen. John, 36
Kennedy, Pres. John F., 156
Ketcham, Rep. John C., 77
Kincheloe, Rep. Dave, 65
Kitchin, Rep. Claude, 33, 35
Krutikov, A. D., USSR, 153, 155
Labor shortage, wartime, 160
Laddie Boy, Harding's dog, 68
Lame Duck Session, 88, 91
Lanham, Rep. Fritz G., 49, 58
Law School, U. of Texas, 82
Leaflets, 1936 campaign, 126
League of Nations, 50, 52
League of Women Voters, 170, 171
Leaving the Congress, 145
Leazer, Jess, Valley View merchant, 129
Lee, Capt. Larry W., 10
Legislative court, 167
Lesley, Charles, 169, 170
Les Miserables, 170
Lever, Rep. Asbury Frank, 36, 37
Lever Food Bill, 1917, 36
Lewisville, Tx., 26
Liberty Loan, 36

Liberty Loan Bill, 1917, 35
Lincoln, Pres. Abraham, 163
Lindsay, Tx., 6
Linthicum, Rep., of Md., 40
Littauer Graduate School, 138, 176
Lodge, Sen. Henry Cabot, 50
Long, Sen. Huey, 102, 124, 182
Longworth House Office Building, 46
Lord, H. C., 169
Lord Manufacturing Co., 169
Los Angeles, Ca., 166
Louisiana riverbed claims, 165
Lowden, Gov. Frank O., 52
Lynch, Donohoe and Dee, 161
Madden, Rep. of Il., 64
Madden, Judge Sam H., 17
Mann, Rep. James R., 42, 43, 49, 51, 175, 181
Marine Band, U. S., 124, 176
Marshall, Gen. George C., 149
Mass distribution, 62
Master, Supreme Court, 165
Master's Report, Sup. Ct., 166
Matador, Tx., 25
Mays, Rep., of Utah, 40, 41
McAdoo, William G., 36, 70, 83, 181
McClintic, Rep. James V., 49
McDade, Noel, 109
McDermott, Mike, 153, 155
McDuffie, John, 115
McNary-Haugen Farm Bill, 77, 78
Mellon, Sec. Andrew, 56
Memphis, Tx., 18
Meredith Dam, 102
Merrit, Charles, 17
Methodist Church, 7
Metze Jones Neely, sister, 1
Mexico, Inaug. of Camacho, 143
Mexico, trip to, 143
Miami, Tx., 9, 14
Miller, Dean Clarence, U. T., 12, 13, 14
Miller, L. D., 17
Mississippi, state riverbed claims, 165
Missouri, University of, 12
Mobilization Committee, 158
Montague County, Tx., 10
Morgan, Rep. Dick T., 53
Morgenthau, Sec. Henry, 88, 90, 113, 182
Mormon Church, 41
Motley County, Tx., 25
Muenster, Tx., 6
Mulhern, J. W., 60
Muniz, Dr. Joao Carlos, of Brazil, 154
Muscle Shoals, 66
Myers, Dean William I., 88, 90, 95, 96, 182
Napoleon, 54
Natchez, Ms., 165
National Judicial Conference, 99
National Livestock Annual Meeting, 105
National Recovery Administration, 98
Neely, Mrs. Jeff M., sister, 1
Neff, Gov. Pat, 57

Nelson, O. H., 15
New congressman, 31
Nieuport, Belgium, 40
Nineteenth Amendment, 39
Ochiltree County, Tx., 17
Office of Price Administration, 148, 149, 150, 151
Oklahoma City, Ok., 166
Oklahoma Panhandle, 15
Oldfield, Rep. William, 45, 47
Olympic, the, 40
Opposition for Congress, 1928, 79
Orlando, Premier, of Italy, 40
Ownby, Joe, 19, 20
Packer Legislation, 1921, 65
Packers and Stockyards Act, 66
Panhandle of Texas, 15, 17, 20, 58, 61, 108, 109
Panhandle Plains Historical Bldg., 96
Panhandle, Tx., 20
Paris Peace Conference, 50
Parity, theory of, 150, 151
Patman, Rep. Wright, 87
Peace comes, 1918, 40
Pearl Harbor, 146
Peary, Charles, hometown banker, 128
Pens used to sign legislation, 96, 143, 144
Pershing, Gen. John J., 40
Peterson, Dr., U. T. law professor, 12
Petrolia, Tx., 58
Piave, River, 40
Pickford, Mary, 36
Plainview, Tx., 28
Plemons, Tx., 18, 20
Poorer cattle, purchase of, 105
Porter, Paul, 126
Post office building plan, 56
Postwar Congress, 1918, 45
Potter County, Tx., 41
Potter, State Sen. C. L., 23
Prescott, Judge William E., 24
President-elect, the, 88
President's official conferences, FDR, 98
Price fixing, 37
Priming the pump, 127
Proctor and Gamble, 158
Production Credit Corporations, 95, 96
Prohibition Amendment, 37, 99
Prohibition, repeal of, 99
Public Lands Com., 106, 107
Public Works Administration, 98
Pump priming, 124
Purnell, Rep. Fred, 75
Quizmaster at U. T., 12, 13
Race for Congress, 22
Railroad Commission, Texas, 61
Railway cars, shortage of, 60
Rainey, Speaker, 115
Rambler, the, 167
Randall County, Tx., 42
Randall, Rep., of Ca., 40
Rankin, Rep. Jeannette, 34, 180
Rankin, Rep. John E., 111, 115, 182

Rayburn, Rep. Sam, 22, 36, 48, 83, 84, 115, 118, 134, 173, 180
Reagan, John H., 61
Reconstruction Finance Corp., 81, 159
Reed, Sen. James A., 50
Reed, Sol.-Gen. Stanley, 118, 174
Reed, Speaker Thomas B., 22
Refinancing farm mortgages, 92
Refinancing Farm Mortgages Act, 98
Regional Agriculture Credit Corp., 95
Rehabilitation Act, 1933, 104
Repeal of prohibition, 99
Republican street parade, 71
Resettlement Administration, 98
Rheims, Cathedral at, 40
Richmond, Va., 166
Ritchie, Gov. Albert C., 70, 83
Rivers and Harbors Committee, 127
Robinson, Sen. Joseph T., 131, 132
Rodman, Admiral, 41
Rogers, Will, 64, 68, 181
Roosevelt, Mrs. Eleanor, 85, 111, 112, 182
Roosevelt, Pres. Franklin D., 6, 37, 52, 70, 83, 84, 85, 86, 87, 100, 109, 114, 132, 143, 145, 152, 153, 154, 162, 163, 176, 182, 183
Ross-Rotan Oratory Prize, 12
Russell, Don, 149
San Francisco, Ca., 166
San Jacinto Society, debating, 10
Sanborn, H. B., 15
Santa Fe Railway, 16, 18
Sawyer, Brig. Gen., 71
Scandals and politics, 69
Schall, Rep. Thomas D., 45
Seibel, Dr. C. W., 58
Senior judge, 163, 167
Senior judge list, 164
Seymour, Tx., 25
Sheppard, Sen. Morris, 44
Sherley, Rep. Swager, 33
Sherman County, Tx., 106
Short, Rep. Dewey, 182
Short, Violet, 28
Should Uncle Sam Pay — When and Why?, 146
Sinclair, Harry, 72
Small lakes, 127
Smith, Gov. Alfred E., 70, 79, 83, 85
Smith, Sen. E. D. "Cotton Ed", 131, 136, 139, 148, 176, 182, 183
Smith, Cotton Ed's Five Year Plan, 103
Snell, Rep. Bert, 113, 175
Soil conservation, 67, 104
Soil Conservation Act, 106, 108, 109, 122, 174, 175
Soil Conservation Service, 108, 155
Soldiers' bonus, 87
Soncy, Tx., 58
Southwestern University, 9, 10, 82
Starnes, Rep. Joe, 127, 177
Star-Telegram, Fort Worth, 57
State, Dept. of, 133, 153
Steagall, Rep. Henry, 93, 94

Stephens, Rep. John H., 24, 26, 28, 29
Stereoscopes, 10
Stevenson, Rep. W. F., 101
Stewart, Mal, 109
Stinnett, A. S. (Syd), 101
Stock market crash, 80
Stone, Justice, 119, 120
Sugar Act, the, 131, 174, 183
Sumners, Rep. Hatton, 48, 89, 174, 181
Supreme Court master, 183
Swift, Louis, 65
Synthetic rubber, 160
Taber, L. J., National Grange, 77
Table quoits, 28
Tammany Hall, 54
Tariff, farmers' share of the, 104, 112
"Tariff," the word, 69
Teapot Dome, 70, 106
Tenant farmers, 124, 128
Tenant Home Purchasing Law, 142
Texas Legislature, 43
Texas Panhandle, 15, 17
Texas Reports, 17
Texas State Fair, 129
Texas Tech University, 57
Thomason, Rep. Robert E., 4, 82
Three-titled bill, 96
Time zones, 42, 181
Timmons, Bascom, 24
Tobey, Charles W., 110
Townes, John C., Law Dean, 12
Trial commissioners, Court of Claims, 164
Tri-State Fair Grounds, 125
Truman, Pres. Harry S, 7, 163
Tulia, Tx., 28
Turkey Track Ranch, 19, 20, 177
Turncoats, Korean War, 167
U-Boats, German, 31
Unanimous Consent Calendar, 43
Underwood, Sen. Oscar W., 70
Underwood, Rip C., 101
University of Texas, 11
Upham, Mark, 158, 159
Usury, in Indian Territory, 21
Valjean, Jean, 170
Valley View, Tx., 1, 4, 10, 28
Vanderbilt University, 11
Vardaman, Sen. James K., 49
Verdun, France, 40
Veterans' hospitals, 41
Vidal, Gore, 64
Vincent, James N., 1905 debater, 10
Vinson, Fred M., 157
Volstead, Andrew J., 99
Wallace, Henry A., 88, 103, 106, 107, 114, 119, 120, 134, 142, 143, 174, 183
Walsh, Sen. Thomas J., 70
War Food Administration, 37, 147, 157
War Food Administrator, 147, 149, 151, 159, 178
Warm Springs, Ga., 88, 90
War Savings Stamps, 1917, 35

Warren, Chief Justice Earl, 163, 167, 183
Washington *Evening Star,* 167
Watson, James, 105
Ways and Means Committee, 131, 132
Welles, Under-Sec. Sumner, 152, 154
Welling, Rep., of Utah, 40, 41
West Texas Chamber of Commerce, 57
Western Headquarters, 1936, 125
Whaley, Chief Judge, Court of Claims, 163
Wheeler, Sen. Burton K., 85
Wheeler, Wayne B., 37
Wichita Falls, Tx., 14, 25
Wickard, Claude, 147, 150, 151, 158
Wilful men, little group of, 32
Williams, Sen. John Sharp, 38
Wilson, M. L., 86, 109
Wilson, Thomas, 65, 66

Wilson, Pres. Woodrow, 31, 32, 38, 45, 50, 52, 54, 180
Wind erosion, 107, 177
Wind erosion conservation districts, 109
Windfall tax, 120, 176
Wizzard Wells, Tx., 27
Woman Suffrage Amendment, 38
Works Progress Administration, 98, 104
World War, 1916, 31
Wood, Gen. Leonard, 52
Woodrum, Cliff, 115
XIT Ranch, 14
Young, Jim, 37
Young, S., Southwestern U., debater, 10
Zeppelin, Ferdinand von, 59

Designed by

EVAN HAYWOOD ANTONE